A Guide to the

Clinical
Use
of the
16 PF

A Guide to the

Clinical Use of the 16 PF

SAMUEL KARSON
and
JERRY W. O'DELL
Eastern Michigan University

Institute for Personality and Ability Testing
Champaign, Illinois 61820

Library of Congress Catalog Card Number: 76-23339
ISBN 0-918296-09-9

Institute for Personality and Ability Testing, Inc.
P. O. Box 188, Champaign, Illinois 61820

Third Printing
Cat. No. LB 284

DEDICATION

To Mary Chasen Libert, an admirable, indomitable personality.

Contents

Contents(*Continued*)

FOREWORD

Until quite recent times, the factor-analytic, experimental exploration of personality structure on the one hand, and the conceptions and measurements used by clinicians on the other, have grown up in two domains with an iron curtain between them. Yet anyone versed in the history of science would realize that since they were converging by different methods upon the same concepts, the practitioners and the researchers must sooner or later get together. However, such an integration called for that rare person among psychologists—an individual thoroughly competent in multivariate experimental methods such as factor analysis and at the same time fully sympathetic to all the needs and practical concerns of the clinical and applied psychologist. Professor Samuel Karson, with the help of Professor O'Dell, has been one of the pioneers who has done so much in the last two decades to bring these two fields together.

The time has come, with the accumulated replication of trait patterns at different ages and across different cultures, when the psychologist needs to understand each pattern and to have a real familiarity with its meaning and predictive power. He is free to take the mathematical foundation on trust, from researches in the field, and to understand these source traits and their operations simply as psychological entities. Unfortunately, in the past he has scarcely

been provided with good textbooks and test handbooks giving
him this real sense of intimacy with the psychological nature of
the structures. This gap is now being filled by the 16 PF Handbook, by numerous journal articles by individual researchers,
and outstandingly by the present book by Professors Karson
and O'Dell, which presents the concepts and their interactions
in terms which any psychologist can follow and enjoy.

The practicing psychologist has to deal with
the individual human being and his most realistic literature is
that of case studies. Drs. Karson and O'Dell follow mainly the
case study approach in this book, showing how particular profiles on the 16 PF have led to particular kinds of behavior in
particular kinds of situations. They also give lively illustrations
of the patterns of certain personality traits in well-known
literary and historical figures. But, to be psychologically
successful in either of these areas of instruction, by actual
cases or by illustrations, the author has to have had exceptional experience with the instruments of measurement for the
basic, primary personality factors. A considerable number of
psychologists in the last decade have begun to acquire that
skill in psychological analysis and most of them find their
whole practice enlightened by the explanatory value of these
concepts. Professor Karson, however, has a truly exceptional
amount of experience in this field, first in clinical work, then in
work for the Federal Aviation Agency, and in the published
research reaching impressive dimensions which he has carried
out personally and inspired in others. The young psychologist
can follow his analyses with some of the appreciation that
young medical students experience in seeing an expert
surgeon wield his scalpel.

A particularly enlightened feature is his integration of the principles of psychodynamics with the interpretation of the measurements of the primary personality factors.
We know today that the basic drives and the sentiment structures built up by learning in the dynamic field are a separate
set of measures from the general personality factors, and they
have in fact been incorporated in recent years in the 10-factor
Motivation Analysis Test. Many psychologists are using the
Motivation Analysis Test and the 16 PF as mutually supple-
mentary areas of information to be integrated in understanding a given case. Although Dr. Karson and Dr. O'Dell have not

brought in measurements by the former instrument, the Motivation Analysis Test, they handle the diagnosis and predictions by the 16 PF with full regard to the drives and acquired interest patterns which interact with the personality factors in the final expressions of behavior. Clinical psychology has developed in many directions, among them being that of behavior therapy employing conditioning principles. However popular this may be at present, it seems most unlikely that the clinician—or any other practicing psychologist—will be able to proceed far without retaining a fundamentally dynamic understanding of human behavior. It is one of the especial virtues of this handling of personality factors by Drs. Karson and O'Dell that they retain and illustrate the dynamic principles which operate along with the personality factors.

The practicing psychologist would be well advised to use this book in conjunction with the Handbook for the 16 PF. The latter contains, to a degree rare among test handbooks, carefully compiled and conveniently listed data on occupational profiles, clinical syndrome diagnoses, and equations for a variety of educational, industrial, and clinical predictions. These can be immediately used statistically by the psychometrist who has access to a computer. But, as stressed in the Handbook, knowledge of the psychology of personality source traits will permit predictions to be carried beyond a merely statistical treatment. The treatment herein is ideally suited to that extension of psychological craftsmanship.

Finally, one must congratulate the authors on having written in a lucid style which every psychologist interested in the field—no matter what his technical specialty—will be able to follow with pleasure.

Raymond B. Cattell

ACKNOWLEDGMENTS

We gratefully express our appreciation to Dorothy Karson and Shirley Bolden of the Ypsilanti Area Public Library for helping us identify certain personality factors with well-known women from real life and fiction. Appreciation is also due Professor Francis Canter of Eastern Michigan University for his valuable suggestions. We must acknowledge our special debt to Dr. H. C. (Pat) Haynes for giving us the opportunity to use the 16 PF in a clinical setting. We also appreciate Professor Raymond B. Cattell's cooperation for permission to quote him liberally in this book.

INTRODUCTION

This book was written in the belief that a simple, elementary guide to the Sixteen Personality Factor Questionnaire (16 PF) would be helpful to practicing clinicians who would like to use this test. The 16 PF is probably one of the best-constructed personality inventories now available to the clinician in his daily work. Despite wide use, it has still not achieved the popularity it deserves among general practitioners. This is partly because the writings of Raymond B. Cattell, the 16 PF's senior author, are technical, mathematical, and geared to a research rather than a clinical audience, but this is perhaps understandable in a scientist of the stature of Cattell. Moreover, the 16 PF is based largely on factor analysis, which most clinicians don't understand very well. Also, the many neologisms such as "premsia," "harria," "sizothymia," "first- and second-stratum factors" (and there are literally hundreds of such terms in Cattell's writings) are sufficient to scare away any but the most ardent technicians, and undoubtedly dissuade them from using the test.

This book assumes that the ideas behind the 16 PF can be expressed in language simple enough to make it attractive and usable to professionals in the field who work with people over 16 years old. The authors' experience over many years, with a large variety of cases, has convinced them that the 16 PF is one of the most useful personality tests currently available. We hope that a reading of this guide will help convince others of this also. It is inevitable that the simple language used here will lose much of the scientific meaning behind the concepts. But, by the same token, it's doubtful that most clinicians know all the subtleties of Freudian terminology (which is at least as complicated as Cattell's), and yet they seem to feel comfortable with it in their daily practice.

1

Administration and Scoring

As we shall see in detail in succeeding chapters, the 16 PF is a questionnaire designed to measure *normal* dimensions of personality. The test provides 16 basic scores for adults. There are other tests available in the same series which allow the testing of younger persons and children. These occasionally include additional scales which are presumed appropriate at only those age levels, and omit some scales that are inappropriate. However, we shall be concerned only with the adult version of the test here.

Available Materials

There are five forms of the 16 PF available. Each form of the test provides the same basic 16 scores which are usually referred to by an alphabetic code such as A, L, or Q_3. The differences among forms stem from the particular testing situations for which each was designed. Form A is the standard version for adults, with Form B being an alternate form for Form A. Forms A and B both consist of 187 items, allowing 10-13 items per scale. Most frequently, the clinician will probably use Forms A and B together in clinical practice.

Forms C and D are similar to Forms A and B, but are designed for rapid occupational selection procedures, and are hence a good deal shorter. They also include a Motivational Distortion (MD) scale to detect attempts at faking good, particularly important in industrial selection situations. The principal objection to Forms C and D is that there are only about seven items on each scale. However, this limitation may have to be lived with in occupational selection situations where time is of great importance.

Form E is intended for people with reading ability below the sixth-grade level. Hence, it is particularly useful with people who have not had the usual educational advantages in our society.

A clinician planning to use the 16 PF should have the following materials at hand:

(1) A copy of the 16 PF *Manual.* This can be gotten as part of the Specimen Set, or separately. It contains complete instructions for administering and scoring the test. However, it does not contain norms or detailed statistical information on the 16 PF. It is meant only as a compact handbook for administrators.

(2) The appropriate *Tabular Supplement* of norms for the form of the 16 PF that one plans to administer. These are not included as part of the manual, since norms are continually being revised to reflect changes in the culture over time. In using this supplement, one must be careful to use the proper table, since there are very many tables in the booklet.

(3) Test booklets. These are reusable when responses are recorded on separate answer sheets.

(4) Enough answer sheets of the proper type for the form of the 16 PF that one wishes to use. Some forms of the 16 PF have answer sheets built into the back of the booklet, but if these answer sheets are used, the booklet is destroyed. However, for one-time test users this can be a real advantage since there is no need to purchase separate answer sheets.

The clinician must immediately decide whether he plans to have the 16 PF machine scored, or whether hand scoring is the method to be used. Both have advantages. If one wants the scores immediately, hand scoring is the only practical method, and one must use hand-scoring answer sheets. However, with hand scoring, it is time consuming to obtain scores on the second-order factors, and other useful scales will probably not be scored, simply because of time limitations.

In most situations, machine scoring is much to be preferred. If machine scoring is to be done, it is particularly important that one obtain the proper answer sheet. Machines cannot score the green hand-scoring sheet. OpScan sheets must be used. These are available from IPAT, which also provides the principal scoring and interpretation services for the 16 PF.

(5) Sufficient profile sheets. If machine scoring is used, the scoring service will provide the proper profile sheet with the scores plotted on it. However, even with machine scoring, it is often handy to have some profile sheets at hand so that one may plot the results in a rather more standard form. Of course, if hand scoring is used, one must have profile sheets. IPAT also offers combination answer-profile sheets which are frequently useful.

(6) Proper scoring keys. These are *not* included in the specimen sets for the 16 PF sold at the present time, since various keys are used for various forms. Forms A and B use the same scoring keys; the other forms have different keys. It is essential that the proper key be used with the proper test. It is wise to keep a spare set of keys available. Colleagues have a way of borrowing scoring keys and not returning them just at the time when they are particularly needed.

(7) A copy of the 16 PF *Handbook*. This is an invaluable source book. Anyone using the 16 PF for any period of time will have frequent recourse to this book.

In addition, one must have sufficient pencils, with erasers, to allow administration of the test. Use of the proper grade of pencil is essential with machine-scoring services.

Administration

Before actual administration can begin, one must decide which form(s) are to be administered. Since the 16 PF, unlike the MMPI, say, does not allow items to appear on more than one scale, there are proportionately fewer items on 16 PF scales. Thus, on Forms A or B, there are between 10 and 13 items per scale. Obviously, it would be wise to have more items.

For this reason, one should administer as many of the forms of the 16 PF as time, and the maintenance of rapport, will allow. Experience has shown that most people will accept taking both Forms A and B with little complaint, and this practice is highly recommended. Other people, with shorter attention spans, will take only Form A, or perhaps only one of the shorter forms (C or D). Those with limited reading skills may have to take Form E. The rule is to give as many items as possible, so as to obtain maximal reliability.

Care should be taken to provide a comfortable, well-ventilated, and properly lighted room. Too often subjects are thrust into the corner of a busy room, where others are talking, and where it is impossible to concentrate. The examiner should take some time to establish rapport with the examinee, so as to allay undue fears about the test and the uses to which the results may be put. Generally, if a full psychological workup is being done, the initial interview will provide an opportunity to establish proper rapport. Ordinarily, patients have few problems completing the 16 PF. The authors can recall only a few incidents over a 20-year period where any problems were encountered in administering the 16 PF. These situations involved older patients who had forgotten their reading glasses! Given proper professional supervision, secretaries have been very successful in administering the 16 PF as part of a test battery; they frequently are unusually good at overcoming initial resistance to the testing procedure.

Detailed instructions for administration are to be found in the 16 PF *Manual,* but we shall summarize them here.

All information on the answer sheet should be filled out; this is especially the case with machine-scoring sheets. In general, the instructions for the 16 PF are quite clearly given on the front of the booklet, and in a sense the test can be said to be self-administering. However, there are always persons who are careless in attending to details of this sort, and if the examiner has the slightest doubt as to whether the examinee understands the instructions, he should not hesitate to make certain that he or she does. The *Manual* suggests that in certain cases the examiner should read the instructions aloud with the examinee. When the examiner is positive that the subject understands the instructions, he may allow him to turn the page and begin.

Normal times for taking the 16 PF are as follows: Forms A and B, about 50 minutes each; Forms C and D, about 30 minutes; and Form E, unspecified. These times should not be taken too literally, however. There is no time limit on the test, and while some people will finish it in a very short time, there will be patients who seem to take forever.

The writers have found that perhaps the most important instruction to give someone taking the test is that of emphasizing that one should not spend a great deal of time on each item, but should give the first response that comes to mind. It is usually sufficient to explain that, while one could easily spend 10 minutes debating the answer to each question, it would then require hours to finish the test. Even such an explanation will not deter the more obsessive patients, and the examiner should set aside sufficient time for stragglers, especially if one is not working with college-educated persons. The *Manual* suggests that, if one wishes to avoid stragglers, one can announce, after a period of 10 minutes or so, that "Most people are now doing question _____."

When the examinees have completed the test, one should collect the booklets, pencils, and answer sheets. Answer sheets should be carefully inspected to make sure that all information is filled in. Invariably, in a group of any size, someone will forget to fill in his or her name. It is particularly important to catch this in the case of answer sheets that will be machine scored.

Machine Scoring

As mentioned, 16 PF answer sheets can be scored either by hand or by machine, *if the proper answer sheet is used.*

Machine scoring has several marked advantages. (1) Scoring services make very few errors, in comparison with human scorers. One hears horror stories about the wholesale errors occasionally made by computers, but in general machine scoring is far more error-free than the human scorer. (2) Machine scoring routinely provides various auxiliary scales and indices. Thus, the second-order factor scores are a standard part of the scoring service output, along with a plot of the scores. Calculation of the second-order scores by machine is very much simplified over the hand method. (3) Scoring machines routinely check for things like multiple marks and omissions; these are all but impossible to detect when the scoring is done by hand. (4) The results from scoring services are generally much more professional looking than those done by a hand scorer.

(5) Most important is the time saving. We have repeatedly seen someone give a class of, say, 50 people both Forms A and B of the 16 PF. Scoring such a number of 16 PF's is a horrendously time-consuming process, taking hours by hand, even if the second-order scores are not calculated. The scoring service eliminates this drudgery, gets the results back in at least the same time, and in the end saves money. Most importantly, far fewer errors are made.

Scoring services certainly earn their fees. They must carefully inspect each answer sheet for improper erasures, spaces not filled in, and the like. The awful things that people can do to machine-scoring answer sheets in filling them in must be seen to be believed. Worse, well-intentioned clinicians frequently give their patients improper information about the proper way to fill in answer sheets, and the scoring service frequently has to fix these errors. It has always been surprising to us that scoring services can do as much as they do for the minimal amount that they charge. Of course, if one has a scoring machine at hand, and a large computer, as is the case with many users in university settings, in-house scoring by machine becomes practical.

If you use a machine-scoring service, a few hints may save you hours of grief. (1) Be sure to use the sort of pencil that the scoring service requires. Most optical scoring machines cannot detect marks made by felt pens, or even ball-point pens. When the scoring service tells you to use a #2 to #2½ pencil, they mean it! The machine may not be sensitive to a harder or softer pencil; worse, a pencil that is too soft may be impossible to erase. (2) Be sure all information is provided. For example, all answer sheets provide a space for the form of the test. The computer has no way of knowing whether the subject has taken Form A, Form B, or whatever, unless that space is filled in. And it is difficult to predict what the computer will decide to do if the form is not specified. It may assume that it is Form A or it may make other assumptions. Only the programmer knows. Similarly, the normative group is frequently not given, and surprisingly often, the name of the examinee is not filled in. (3) Be sure that the forms do not have stray marks on them. Often the subject will circle troublesome items for later reference; if these marks are not erased before scoring, the machine may pick them up as valid marks. (4) Finally, to repeat, be certain that the answer sheet that you are using is the proper one for the scoring service that you're using. If you use the wrong form, you'll either have to copy over all the items to the proper sheets, or change scoring services.

In addition to the essentially clerical tasks of adding items together to form scale scores and converting raw scores to standard scores, the computer is capable of analyzing score patterns and generating complete interpretive reports as well. In some cases,[1] it has been difficult, if not impossible, to tell whether a particular report was produced by machine or not! In many cases, computer interpretation goes hand in hand with computer scoring, and that pattern is likely to become even more common in the future as psychological technology makes further advances.

Hand Scoring

Hand scoring is appropriate if you have only a few 16 PF's to score, and if you need them in a hurry. The 16 PF *Manual* is quite clear on the subject of scoring, and the precise details will vary with the form of the test being used. In general, one first puts the scoring template on the answer sheet. The trick here is to be sure that the little star on the answer sheet shows through the template. One then scores

---

[1]Karson, S., & O'Dell, J. W. A new automated interpretation system for the 16 PF. *Journal of Personality Assessment*, 1975, *39*(3), 256-260.

each scale, adding the correct number of points specified by each hole in the template. Generally, two templates are used for each form to avoid crowding on the templates. When scoring of the answer sheet is completed, you should have the raw scores written in the boxes on the right-hand side of the sheet. It is then important that you *check* your scoring. Many people feel that errors cannot crop up in such a simple process, but the authors find that they routinely make at least one mistake in hand scoring for each record.

Looking up the Norms

When the answer sheet has been scored, you have the *raw* scores for the 16 scales. These must be converted to the sort of standard scores used on the 16 PF, which are called "stens," meaning "standard ten." Stens are standard scores with a mean of 5.5, a standard deviation of 2, and range from 1 to 10. These scores are very convenient to use, and the 16 PF profile sheet makes it quite clear where the average falls, when they are plotted.

Determining sten scores is quite simple. One simply defines the normative group that one wishes to use, say, "High School Juniors and Seniors," "College Students," or "General Population." Then one looks in the appropriate Tabular Supplement for the proper stens corresponding to the raw scores that one has gotten. At the present writing, "Tabular Supplement Number 1" is current for Forms A and B, but it is likely to be replaced in time by more up-to-date supplements.

Keep in mind that stens gotten from the Tabular Supplements are given with reference to the group named. That is, someone compared with the General Population on the intelligence (B) scale will tend to get a higher score than he would if compared with College Students on the same scale. It should also be kept in mind that the *raw* scores on the scales are meaningless; only the stens are referenced against a comparison group, and are thus usable.

The stens should then be transferred to a profile sheet and plotted. Stens of 5 or 6 are considered average. A sten of 4 or 7 would be considered slightly deviant from the norm; 2, 3, 8, and 9 are strongly deviant, while stens of 1 or 10 are considered extreme, since they occur so rarely in adults.

Supplementary Scales

It may well be that the problem most unique to personality testing lies in the fact that people taking personality tests tend to attempt to present a false picture of themselves, whether through direct faking, careless answering, or in other ways. It is important that we have means available for the detection of such deception.

In principle, there are three sorts of faking that may occur. In the first, people may attempt to "fake good," to make themselves look better on a test than they really do. In the 16 PF literature, faking good has been called "Motivational Distortion," usually abbreviated as "MD." In other situations, people will attempt to look as bad as possible. It is wise to have a means available to check for such faking. Finally, it is a frequent occurrence that examinees will attempt to get around a personality test by simple random answering. This too must be detected.

Forms C and D of the 16 PF have a specific Motivational Distortion (MD) scale built into them. This MD scale is scored along with the other scales, and may be interpreted along with the appropriate Tabular Supplement for those forms.

However, Forms A and B are more widely used, and no MD scale exists for these scales. As a result, the writers have found it necessary to develop some special scales, specifically for Form A, which will allow the detection of Motivational Distortion, Faking Bad, and Random answering. These scales are described in Appendix A, along with instructions for scoring them.

The effects of various sorts of response sets on the 16 PF on the profile itself are interesting to note. Obviously, random answering should result in a rather flat 16 PF profile, because of the balanced way in which the 16 PF items are written, and such is the case, except for the intelligence (B) scale, in which the score will drop dramatically.

Figure 1-1 shows the results of radical sets to fake good and fake bad. Notice that scales E (dominance), I (emotional sensitivity), M (imaginativeness), N (shrewdness), Q_1 (rebelliousness), and Q_2 (self-sufficiency) appear to be immune to distortion, either from faking good or faking bad. The scales which seem to be particularly subject to distortion

FIGURE 1-1
EFFECTS OF FAKING GOOD AND FAKING BAD
RESPONSE SETS

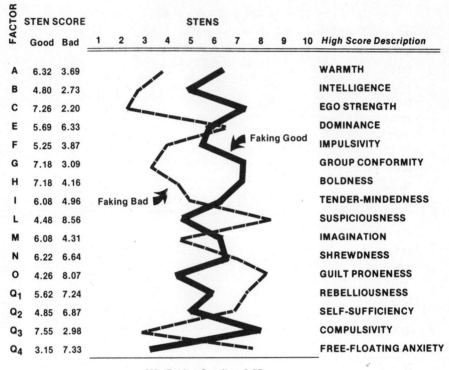

FACTOR	STEN SCORE		STENS										High Score Description
	Good	Bad	1	2	3	4	5	6	7	8	9	10	
A	6.32	3.69											WARMTH
B	4.80	2.73											INTELLIGENCE
C	7.26	2.20											EGO STRENGTH
E	5.69	6.33											DOMINANCE
F	5.25	3.87											IMPULSIVITY
G	7.18	3.09											GROUP CONFORMITY
H	7.18	4.16											BOLDNESS
I	6.08	4.96											TENDER-MINDEDNESS
L	4.48	8.56											SUSPICIOUSNESS
M	6.08	4.31											IMAGINATION
N	6.22	6.64											SHREWDNESS
O	4.26	8.07											GUILT PRONENESS
Q_1	5.62	7.24											REBELLIOUSNESS
Q_2	4.85	6.87											SELF-SUFFICIENCY
Q_3	7.55	2.98											COMPULSIVITY
Q_4	3.15	7.33											FREE-FLOATING ANXIETY

MD (Faking Good) = 9.57
MD (Faking Bad) = 3.31

Source: Winder, O'Dell, & Karson (1975). Copyright 1975 by the Society for Personality Assessment, Inc. Reprinted by permission.

are C (ego strength), G (group conformity), L (suspiciousness), O (guilt proneness), Q3 (ability to bind anxiety), and Q4 (free-floating anxiety), which, as we shall see, are almost all measures of anxiety on the 16 PF.

The MD scale for the 1967 Form A of the 16 PF (Winder, O'Dell, & Karson, 1975), having been scored as shown in the Appendix, must then be interpreted. The writers have found that a raw score of 6 or more on this scale should be looked at with suspicion; this is because the average score on the MD scale is about 4. When one encounters an MD score as high as 12 or so, one can be almost certain that there is a conscious attempt to fake.

Similarly, the Faking Bad scale, having been scored, is considered suspicious if it exceeds 6 in raw-score form, since the average score is about 2. Again, a score as high as 12 is presumptive evidence of faking.

Finally, the Random scale raw score is considered suspect if it reaches 5 or more. Similarly to the others, if this scale reaches 12, there can be little doubt that something strange is going on. However, it could be only that the subject did not clearly understand the instructions for the test. In any event, a check should be made.

It is strongly recommended that the MD, Faking Bad, and Random scores be routinely obtained on any 16 PF whenever possible. This procedure is especially crucial when the questionnaire is given in a selection situation, in which the subject perceives that he or she stands to gain or lose something on the basis of the test results. Scoring for response sets is particularly essential in situations where the interpreter does not have the chance to see the subject in person, but is only interpreting the results of a test given by someone else.

2

An Example of a 16 PF Interpretation

The 16 PF was constructed to cover the whole range of adult personality. However, we shall assume that clinicians are largely interested in getting at the pathological rather than the normal aspects of a subject's personality, and will accordingly slant our comments in that direction. But it should be realized that the 16 PF, unlike many other tests, allows for the detection and description of normal personality. On tests such as the MMPI, a patient is forced into categories like "schizophrenic" or "nonschizophrenic." If he does not fall into any of the clinical categories, there may be little that one can say about his personality functioning without a great deal of deductive reasoning. On the 16 PF, even if a patient is not grossly disturbed, one can still say a good deal about the dynamics of his personality. As an illustration, let us turn our attention to a 16 PF profile interpretation.

In Figure 2-1 we show the 16 PF profile of an unusual case. The person in question was a 33-year-old man, in a highly responsible position, who was referred for evaluation because of difficulties at work. Pertinent details have been changed for ethical reasons. The clinical report generated read as follows:

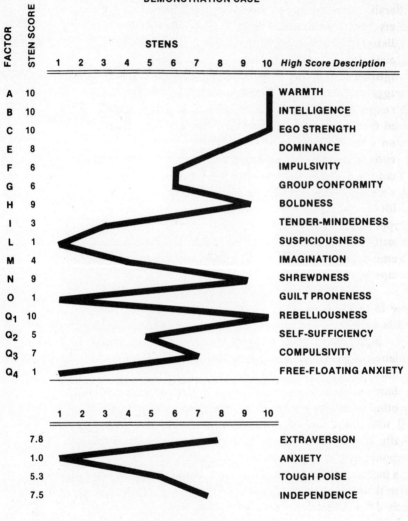

FIGURE 2-1
DEMONSTRATION CASE

FACTOR	STEN SCORE	STENS	High Score Description
A	10		WARMTH
B	10		INTELLIGENCE
C	10		EGO STRENGTH
E	8		DOMINANCE
F	6		IMPULSIVITY
G	6		GROUP CONFORMITY
H	9		BOLDNESS
I	3		TENDER-MINDEDNESS
L	1		SUSPICIOUSNESS
M	4		IMAGINATION
N	9		SHREWDNESS
O	1		GUILT PRONENESS
Q_1	10		REBELLIOUSNESS
Q_2	5		SELF-SUFFICIENCY
Q_3	7		COMPULSIVITY
Q_4	1		FREE-FLOATING ANXIETY

7.8		EXTRAVERSION
1.0		ANXIETY
5.3		TOUGH POISE
7.5		INDEPENDENCE

MD = 10

16

A review of this profile shows high scores on warmth (A), ego strength (C), rebelliousness (Q_1), and leadership, and minimum scores on guilt proneness (O), anxiety, and neuroticism. The MD of 10 indicates that this is a distorted profile, at least in regard to anxiety factors L (suspiciousness), Q_4 (free-floating anxiety), C (ego strength), and O (guilt proneness). His Factor B score of 10 suggests an extremely intelligent individual who tends to be especially critical and rebellious, with a strong unresolved Oedipal complex ($Q_1 = 10$). He is an extraverted person with some propensity for acting out his conflicts. He tends to be dominant and aggressive (E = 8), far more so than the average worker. His high score of 9 on N suggests a shrewd and calculating individual, much of whose hostility is channeled into intellectual paths as well as into interpersonal relationships. One wonders why the necessity to deny anxiety so strongly and to such an extreme degree. One also wonders about the adequacy of his superego controls (O = 1).

It is believed he would be especially troublesome to supervisors or to anyone in authority over him. This is seen in his personality programming, namely, his very high intelligence and his strong rebellious tendencies. His relatively low scores on I and M suggest that he is a tough, practical individual, characteristics that he shares with the majority of people in his profession. On the other hand, the score of 10 on A does not seem to fit well with his I and M scores inasmuch as low scores usually go together on A, I, and M. But he has the maximum score possible on A and it may either be faked or an indication that he achieves much dependency gratification through social interaction. His H of 9 is also significantly different from his peer group and suggests that he is a high risk-taker with much overt interest in the opposite sex. In short, he is a bold, adventurous person who has all the earmarks of being a good con-man; that is, psychopathic qualities would not be unexpected in such a person. He has the necessary shrewdness to attempt to carry off some grand schemes. This is certainly one of the most unusual profiles I have seen on any person in his profession.

This interpretation was done blindly, and the results returned to the agency requesting the evaluation. It must be admitted that we were surprised at the follow-up we obtained from the referring psychiatrist:

Enclosed are my comments on the interpretation sent to us the other day. This man has been with the company since 1968, and probably had experience with the same kind of job in the military. In any event, he is the rather infamous man who got on TV and described his company's operation in Boston as a "killer plant," criticizing it (rather unjustly, I think) as emitting too much pollution. Both the personnel director and the president of our company were flabbergasted that the test, in competent hands, could yield so much accurate information about a person.

We can't claim that one has this kind of luck every day with the 16 PF, but it does show that the test can be an invaluable tool.

Let us look at the profile in Figure 2-1 in detail, along with the report generated, taking the latter apart piece by piece:

A review of this profile shows high scores on warmth (A), ego strength (C), rebelliousness (Q$_1$), and leadership, and minimum scores on guilt proneness (O), anxiety, and neuroticism.

The derivation of this is simple, the profile merely being scanned to get a general idea of the scatter. Since the 16 PF scores are reported as "stens" (standard scores with a mean of 5.5 and a standard deviation of 2) it should be obvious that scores of 10 or 1, which are obtained by only 2.3% of the people taking the test, are quite rare. But this patient has seven scores of this statistical rarity! Surely there is something unusual either about him or his way of responding. How can we determine what it is?

The MD of 10 indicates that this is a distorted profile, at least in regard to anxiety factors L (suspiciousness), Q$_4$ (free-floating anxiety), C (ego strength), and O (guilt proneness).

The MD or motivational distortion score is a measure of one's tendency to "fake good" on the 16 PF, and his score of 10 is a great deal higher than the average score on this scale (about 4). Thus, it is a safe bet that the man was trying to put himself in a good light, trying to avoid giving answers which would indicate disturbance. The scales most indicative of disturbance on the 16 PF are C (ego strength), L (suspiciousness), O (guilt proneness), Q_4 (free-floating anxiety), and the second-order factors measuring anxiety and neurotic trend. Thus, our original suspicion about the possibility of faking good seems borne out, since our subject would have us believe that he has almost perfect ego strength (C = 10), suspects nothing about anyone (L = 1), has no guilt at all (O = 1), almost no anxiety (Q_4 = 1, second-order anxiety = 1), and has no tendency toward neuroticism (neuroticism = 1). Thus, he was clever enough to be able to fake all of the scores which would make him look bad in any way. But, since it is doubtful that anyone is that perfect, his very success in doing so has tripped him up. At the same time, it is likely that he must be very clever to be such a successful faker. The major question which must now be resolved is that of whether he has faked so much that the whole record must be considered totally invalid.

The question of whether to reject the profile as totally faked can be resolved immediately if we find that he says anything about himself which is unflattering, and he does. He would have us believe that he is a very venturesome individual, more so than about 93% of the population (H = 9), that he is equally shrewd (N = 9), and extremely critical and rebellious (Q_1 = 10). No one would admit to these tendencies if he were trying to appear to be an ideal human being; thus he was faking mainly with regard to those things which might lead us to suspect classic neurotic or psychotic trends. At the same time, a picture of the man's character begins to emerge, since we know that he is skilled at putting himself in a good light, that he is extraverted (extraversion = 7.8), outgoing (A = 10), venturesome and socially bold (H = 9), shrewd and calculating (N = 9), radical (Q_1 = 10), and would have us believe that he has great leadership potential (leadership = 10). He is higher than about 90 % of the population on these characteristics, and, considering that he is rather tough-minded

(I = 3) and practical (M = 4), an ordinary knowledge of personality dynamics would suggest that he probably has sociopathic tendencies. A man who was trying to fake on all counts certainly would not admit to these trends in his personality, hence we may assume that the record is worthy of serious interpretation. But we know that he can fake very well when he wants to. Consequently we must assume that the sociopathic trends in his personality are acceptable to him. This, of course, is the classic definition of a sociopath. We shall keep this as a working assumption, and return to the analysis of the rest of the report.

His Factor B score of 10 suggests an extremely intelligent individual....

The B (intelligence) scale of the 16 PF consists of 26 items, if both Forms A and B of the test are given, as they were in this instance. Since his score is higher than about 97% of the population, it is not unwarranted to assume that he is quite intelligent. And he must be bright to fake so effectively.

... who tends to be especially critical and rebellious, with a strong unresolved Oedipal complex ($Q_1 = 10$).

This is a reference to his score, the highest possible (10), on Q_1, generally dubbed "rebelliousness." Q_1 is one of the more crucial scores on the 16 PF. Someone with a high score on this scale is admitting to a very troublesome character trait. Such a person feels that money can buy almost everything, that society would be much better off if it threw away its old habits and traditions, and that he is not bothered if someone thinks him unconventional or odd. In moderation such tendencies may be good, but carried to extremes they suggest a person who is difficult to get along with, one in disagreement with society about virtually everything. The inference that such a person has an unresolved Oedipal complex follows from Freudian theory.

He is an extraverted person with some propensity for acting out his conflicts.

This inference was made from the fact that he has a very high second-order extraversion score, higher than about 87% of the population. The score of 10 on Factor A, the "outgoing-reserved" dimension, would not in itself indicate acting out; it would suggest that he was merely a warm, outgoing person. The second-order extraversion score, however, elevated as highly as it is, and coupled with high dominance (E = 8) and above average immaturity (F = 6), suggests that he is more than merely outgoing. His outgoingness has a hostile, active edge to it, and hence the inference that he acts out his impulses. This is also shown by the following comment:

He tends to be dominant and aggressive (E = 8), far more so than the average worker.

This is a direct interpretation of his high score on Factor E, or "dominance, aggressiveness, assertiveness, stubbornness, and competitiveness." He may be outgoing, but one had better watch out for him, or he'll take over the situation. The comment that:

His high score of 9 on N suggests a shrewd and calculating individual, much of whose hostility is channeled into intellectual paths as well as into interpersonal relationships

further reinforces the interpretation being developed. A score on N, or "shrewdness, calculatingness, and worldliness" of 9, higher than 93% of the population, indicates that he is well aware of how to deal with the world around him, of how to manage people and situations. High N implies having sufficient intelligence to carry out these aspirations, and we know that our patient has more than enough of this. He begins to look more and more like a manipulator.

One wonders why the necessity to deny anxiety so strongly and to such an extreme degree.

This is an obvious conclusion. If this man is so good at managing the world, as shown by his effectiveness in faking the anxiety scores and the other factors commented on, he would be shrewd enough to know that his extreme denial of anxiety would be picked up. Surely, this must be a chink in his otherwise hard armor. The implication is strong that, while he is generally successful in working the world around to his designs, there are times when he extends himself a bit too far in this fashion, beyond his capacity to handle the bluff successfully. What is he bluffing about? We can't know directly, but it is a reasonable hypothesis that deep-seated anxiety underlies his approach to the 16 PF. At the same time, it is equally reasonable that, with his generally successful defensive structure, we're going to have a very difficult time finding out what lies beneath it. If we could study his personality in depth, through a complete psychological and psychiatric workup, we might learn more about his underlying dynamics. But, if he could fake successfully on the 16 PF, he might well be able to sail through a complete psychiatric examination almost as easily. Thus, one might have to resort to long-term psychotherapy to learn much about him. But, in view of his personality structure, it is unlikely that one could get him to agree to this.

One also wonders about the adequacy of his superego controls ($O = 1$).

Although his score on the group conformity factor, G, is higher than average, notice that his score on Factor O, guilt proneness, is the lowest possible score. G and O are the scores that one looks at to evaluate the effectiveness of the superego controls along with F (impulsivity) and Q_3 (obsessiveness). While he is high average on group conformity (on the basis of G), he has so little tendency to feel guilt (O) that we must question the strength of his internalized superego. One must feel a bit of guilt to get along in the world, and he says that he feels none. Beyond this, the general picture of sociopathic trends that he has been showing further casts doubt on his superego controls. After all, a man who answers that "In a situation which may become dangerous, I believe in making a fuss and speaking up even if calmness and politeness are lost" (a scale-N item), who shows tendencies toward radicalism (Q_1), devil-may-care adventuresomeness (high H), and dominance (high E), would not seem to be someone with a strong superego, even though the other scores might suggest it.

The second paragraph of the interpretation sums up what has been said so far:

It is believed he would be especially trouble- some to supervisors or to anyone in authority over him. This is seen in his personality programming, namely, his very high intelligence and his strong rebellious tenden- cies. His relatively low scores on I and M suggest that he is a tough, practical individual, characteristics that he shares with the majority of people in his profession.

Clearly, he is bright, from the score on scale B (intelligence), and he admits to being quite radical and rebellious, with the highest possible score on Q_1. Such a person would disagree with his supervisors frequently, and have the intelligence to make it stick, along with the aggres- siveness (high E) to make the dispute annoying. He clearly would rather be a supervisor than be supervised. The fact that low scores on I (toughness) and M (practicality) are also present further suggests that he would be willing to stand up for his rights, again hinting that he would not back down easily in a squabble with his superiors.

On the other hand, the score of 10 on A does not seem to fit well with his I and M scores inasmuch as low scores usually go together on A, I, and M. But he has the maxi- mum score possible on A and it may either be faked or an indication that he achieves much dependency gratification through social interaction.

It is a statistical fact that A, I, and M usually vary together, since they appear together on a second-order factor (to be discussed in Chapter 5), and consequently a deviation of the magnitude found between I and M, which are both low, compared to A, which has the highest score possible, is most unusual. Since there is a strong likelihood that this man has faked his profile, the high A may only be an attempt to look good. If it is not faked, one would have to accept the idea that the usual interpretation of A (warmth) is the correct one. The latter seems unlikely in view of the high scores already mentioned on the hostility indicators, E and Q_1.

His H of 9 is also significantly different from his peer group and suggests that he is a high risk-taker with much overt interest in the opposite sex. In short, he is a bold,

adventurous person who has all the earmarks of being a good con-man; that is, psychopathic qualities would not be unexpected in such a person. He has the necessary shrewdness to attempt to carry off some grand schemes. This is certainly one of the most unusual profiles I have seen on any person in his profession.

Brief mention has already been made concerning the role of scale H (boldness) in 16 PF profile interpretation. It indicates venturesomeness and interest in people. The remainder of the paragraph sums up what we have already guessed, namely, that the patient has a streak of the sociopath in him. Look at the evidence which may be marshalled to support this view: he has almost certainly faked the profile to suit his ends, and yet he has done it selectively, suggesting great skill in manipulation. However, he did it a bit too well, which indicates that his very success at manipulating outcomes may trip him up at times. While he has managed to deny almost everything about himself which might suggest neurotic or psychotic conditions, he did not see fit to deny character problems, showing that he does not feel them to be either socially objectionable or incompatible with his ego ideal. Consequently, he admits to a good deal of aggressiveness and dominance, a rather ruthless venturesomeness, unusual cleverness, and great rebelliousness and radicalism. Further, he is bright, which gives him a good deal to work with in carrying out his schemes, assuming our hypothesis to be correct. Finally, he admits to no guilt feelings at all, which, if true, would fit nicely into the classic picture of the sociopath.

While this interpretation was made on a very unusual profile, it should be clear by now that the 16 PF can provide a great deal of information to someone with a basic understanding of its workings. Granted, it does require thought on the part of the person making the interpretation. The 16 PF does not provide a direct diagnosis of sociopathic tendencies, as the MMPI sets out to do. The interpreter must take the indications given him by the 16 PF, and, through his knowledge of personality dynamics, develop a conception of the person he is dealing with. This is not actuarial prediction, but it most certainly is in the best tradition of clinical practice.

3

The Construction
of the 16 PF

We do not propose to go deeply into the construction of the 16 PF, but the way in which it was put together is so unique that it is impossible to resist discussing the process a little.[1]

Professor Cattell's major purpose in constructing the test was to provide an instrument which would measure the most fundamental dimensions of normal personality and comprehensively span the entire range of personality characteristics in adults. The initial problem was that of finding a set of descriptive categories sufficiently wide to take in the many, many variations of human personality. There would seem to be an almost infinite number of ways to complete this description. Take, for example, literary characters: Hamlet was indecisive and probably Oedipal, Othello was inordinately jealous, Iago was malicious and self-seeking, Tristram Shandy was capricious, Tristan and Isolde were unduly passionate, and Heathcliffe simply puzzling in his hostility. The ways in which human personality may be described seem so varied as to make any systematization of them impossible.

The really clever thing about the construction of the 16 PF, and, it might be added, many of the other tests in Cattell's armamentarium, was that he was able to see the

[1] The nontechnically minded reader should feel free to skip this chapter; it is not necessary to be familiar with it to interpret the 16 PF.

forest for the trees. For it should be obvious that there really is not an infinite number of ways in which people can be described. There are only the ways for which the English language provides words, specifically adjectives, and one can obtain a complete listing of all these words at the local bookstore in what is called a "dictionary." In the dictionary, one will find all the subtleties of expression that the language can produce. The words attached to the literary characters mentioned above are all present: "indecisive," "jealous," "self-seeking," "capricious," "passionate," and "hostile" are all in the dictionary. And, to simplify the problem, Allport and Odbert in 1936 combed the dictionary and listed all the adjectives which could be found which applied to human personality. Thus, in about 4,000 words gotten by Allport and Odbert, we have a good sampling of all the ways in which one person may describe another's personality. The seemingly infinite number of ways in which personality could be characterized seems to boil down, really, to about 4,000. Granted, there may be unconscious, unknowable things about people not yet represented in the dictionary. But if concepts have not officially entered the language yet, it would be very difficult to communicate them in a psychological report.

Cattell proposed to use the personality-descriptive adjectives in the very language we speak as the starting place for his test; in this way he would run little risk of missing any of the possible nuances of human psychological processes.

The problem, however, was that a list of 4,000 adjectives remains an enormous number of concepts to deal with. It is reasonable that this number could be substantially reduced; the existence of great numbers of synonyms in the English language implies this. Cattell's immediate problem, then, was that of discovering a systematic way of reducing the 4,000 adjectives to a manageable number. But how to do this?

Happily, by the 1940's, when this development was proceeding, a technique called factor analysis had been fairly well perfected by Spearman, Thomson, Holzinger, Thurstone, and other workers. We won't claim here that factor analysis can be easily understood in all its details, for it builds upon the work of some of the most distinguished and sophisticated mathematicians that ever lived. But it is, in broad outline, a technique with a very simple purpose.

Take, for example, Cattell's problem of somehow getting the 4,000 adjectives into a more manageable form. It is reasonable to assume that one could account for most of the information contained in the 4,000 adjectives with a smaller number of concepts. For example, words like extraverted, outgoing, adaptable, expressive, cooperative, and others would all seem to have a good deal in common. If somehow a way could be found to establish scientifically that they are related, we could replace these five words by one single concept, thus reducing the 4,000 adjectives to 3,996. If this could be done throughout the list of words (and a certain amount of progress could be made through the use of synonyms), it stands to reason that a great saving in the number of concepts could be achieved. However, doing it merely by inspection would not be the best method, for eventually one would run into situations where a decision as to which word to include in a given concept would be very difficult. For this reason, a systematic method is needed, and for a problem of this size, it is not difficult to realize that "systematic" is going to imply "logical" or "mathematical." Logic and mathematics were proved to be identical by Bertrand Russell at the turn of the century, so that there is no conflict between the terms.

Think for a moment about what the basic problem to be solved in reducing the 4,000 words is going to be. "Reducing" suggests that we are going to go from 4,000 words to a lesser number of concepts. The obvious question is that of how many concepts the "lesser number" will have to be. Will it be 3,999, ..., 1,000, ..., 25, ..., or perhaps only 1? All of these are perfectly possible, and it should be apparent that the major problem to be solved in any reductive or factor analytic procedure is simply that of discovering how few concepts one can reduce things to, while still accounting for most of the original information. In short, the basic problem of factor analysis is that of deciding what the precise, smaller number of factors will be that will be required to account for the larger number of variables or factors, in this case, 4,000.

If you dislike mathematics, you should be happy to hear that there is no really definitive way to solve this problem, but there are many approximations or guesses that are used to make the decision. Then, once one has determined how few factors one can get away with, the remaining problem is that of the relationship of the smaller number of factors to the larger number of descriptors. These two problems—(1) finding out how few factors are needed to account for the larger number of variables, and (2) finding the relationship of the larger number of variables to the smaller number of factors—are the two basic problems that must be solved in any factor analysis.

There is little point in going into technical details about how the process is accomplished, for there are many ways of gaining the two objectives, and none of them has a clear-cut advantage over the others. Moreover, there are new ways constantly being developed. If you'd like a name to identify the process, the method most frequently used is called the principal axis method. It has a long history of development in other areas of science, but it is by no means the only method of accomplishing a factor analysis.

Returning to Cattell's problem of determining a method to reduce the 4,000 words to the basic, underlying dimensions or factors of human personality, he proceeded as follows: It would have been nice to throw the 4,000 adjectives into the factor analysis procedure and let it decide which underlying elements could be used to account for the data, but there was one very large fly in the ointment. This obstacle was the simple fact that doing a factor analysis on even 100 variables in the 1940's was a sheer, physical impossibility. The computations involved are extremely lengthy, repetitious, and boring in any factor analysis. It was not uncommon in those days to have several people, working five days a week, eight hours a day, take about three years to handle 40 variables, and even then the method used was only an approximation to the desired procedure. With the advent of computers, the problem has been alleviated to a great extent, but it would still be essentially impossible to factor all 4,000 adjectives. At any rate, when Cattell began his researches, he had to group his 4,000 words, pretty much by sophisticated inspection, into 180 categories. These were reduced by correlational methods to 45 categories. The 45 categories could be handled by the methods available at the time, and were factor analyzed. Details of the process may be found in Cattell (1973).

The outcome of Cattell's analysis of the language was that there appeared to be 12 to 15 factors underlying the description of personality in the English language, and these were named, simply, A through O. As one proceeds through the alphabet, these factors decrease somewhat in their importance, although all remain useful. Thus, Factor A (warmth) is first in importance, Factor B (intelligence) is second, Factor C (ego strength) is third, and so on. This tallies well with everyday observation, for warmth, intelligence, and ego strength would be acknowledged by most psychologists to be of primary importance in human personality. We shall get into precise definitions of the factors later on, in the next chapter. But, to repeat, Cattell felt that he had successfully reduced personality descriptions in the English language to 15 dimensions. As it turned out, some of the basic factors did not prove to be very replicable in adults—namely, D, J, and K—and you'll observe that these are missing from the 16 PF.

You have probably noticed that there are four factors on the 16 PF profile sheet which we haven't mentioned, specifically Q_1, Q_2, Q_3, and Q_4. These are factors which are found only in questionnaires, that is, the usual paper-and-pencil inventories that most of us use. They did not turn up in the analysis of the language, but they seemed important in everyday life, and Cattell felt that they should be included in the test. Since questionnaires are clearly more subject to faking than other ways of measuring personality, and thus provide somewhat less satisfactory data, Cattell felt that the "Q" factors should be distinguished from the factors discovered from the language analysis. He therefore called them "Q" factors, simply numbered them, and put them at the end of the list. However, the "Q" factors have turned out to be much more valuable than originally thought. You will find in the cases at the end of the book that they are given an equal ranking with the other factors. But the "Q" designation remains.

4

The Scales of the 16 PF

We shall now describe the scales of the 16 PF, beginning with the first-order factor scales, followed by the second-order scales. The materials for the description of the scales were taken from virtually all the many writings on the 16 PF, especially the 16 PF *Handbook* (Cattell, Eber, & Tatsuoka, 1970) and Cattell's two other major sources on the test, *Personality and Motivation Structure and Measurement* (1957) and *Personality and Mood by Questionnaire* (1973). The bibliography lists other source writings on the test.

The books mentioned to this point have certain deficiencies for our purpose, however: their focus is more on the description of personality in general than on the clinical application of the test. To obtain information about clinical uses, an interesting procedure was used by the writers. About 100 blind interpretations made by the senior author were collected over a period of several months. Each interpretation was then content analyzed in a crude way, and every statement made about every characteristic of the patient was written down on an index card together with the 16 PF scale scores which led to the interpretation. The cards were then sorted into piles by scales, and each pile was ordered with regard to the magnitude of the scores. For example, there was a pile of statements made, using the scores on scale A, and these were sorted so that we had a complete listing of comments made on that scale. An abbreviated version of the comments for scale A follows:

Sten Score	Comment
1	He is an extremely introverted person.
1	Marked introverted tendencies.
1	He seems to be a person with very little warmth who probably has a history of early conflictual family relations which has resulted in a marked turning away from people.
4	Somewhat reserved person.
7	His high A indicates an outgoing and warm individual.
10	Extremely extraverted personality structure.

By this process we achieved an objective compilation of one clinician's interpretation of the scales. This filled in the gaps in many of the 16 PF texts, where abnormal characteristics, while not ignored, are mixed in with interpretations primarily of interest in the study of normal personality. Over a thousand such interpretations were garnered in this way from the 100 blind interpretations which had been collected, so that an extensive library of comments was formed. These comments are often incorporated in the scale descriptions which follow.

A word about the format of the 16 PF scales is in order. If you refer back to Figure 2-1, you'll notice that almost all of the 16 PF scales are bipolar. That is, they have two ends to them. For example, scale N has as its higher end shrewdness, and as its lower end, naivete. This is in direct contrast to many personality tests now in current usage, which allow a subject only to be *high* on a given trait. The MMPI scales, for example, permit a patient only to be a hypochondriac, depressive, or whatever. The status of low scores on the MMPI scales is unclear. We regard it as a marked superiority of the 16 PF that both ends of the scales are interpretable. There is virtually always something to comment on about every factor. On the intelligence scale, B, it is stretching things to think of a two-ended scale; but the 16 PF authors decided that it would be too confusing to intermix unipolar and bipolar scales and so show all scales with two poles.

As mentioned in an earlier chapter, all the scales on the 16 PF are shown as "standard-ten" or "sten" scores, implying that there are ten possible gradations on the scales. These scales are normalized (adjusted to fit the normal curve) standard scores, with a mean of 5.5 and a standard deviation of 2. In general, primary sten scores are not expressed with numbers after the decimal point.[1] This is good practice, since most personality tests, including the 16 PF, do not provide meaningful differentiations at more than ten levels.

Each item on the 16 PF has three possible answers. Except for scale B (intelligence), which simply adds 1 point for each correct answer, the items are scored so that either the first or last alternative counts 2 raw-score points and the center alternative always counts 1 point. Thus, each item may be keyed 2 for the first alternative, 1 for the second, and 0 for the third, or else, 0 for the first alternative, 1 for the second, and 2 for the third. These are referred to for brevity as 2,1,0 or 0,1,2 items. The 16 PF was constructed with the problems of response sets clearly in mind, so that there are generally equal numbers of 2,1,0 and 0,1,2 items on each scale.

We shall begin the description of the scales at this point. First we present the adjectives from the 16 PF *Handbook* which are used to define the factor. This will be followed by comments about what it is that each scale measures, based on our own clinical and research experience as well as Cattell's writings. It is strongly recommended that the student consult a copy of the 16 PF *Handbook*, especially pages 80 to 109, when reading this section. It is also urged that the reader look up the items on each scale while learning about it. This can be done by referring to the 16 PF Tabular Supplement (IPAT Staff, 1970), where the numbers of the items on

---

[1]Second-order factor scores on the 16 PF are usually calculated to one decimal place. This is largely an historical accident, but one can argue that the second-order scores, since they are calculated as combinations of the primary scales and are thus more reliable, are entitled to be reported more precisely than the primaries.

each scale and their scoring direction are listed. These numbered items can easily be compared against the questionnaire booklet to find the actual items on the scale.

Please note that the factor names we have chosen here are not always exactly those given in the 16 PF *Handbook*. We tried to use titles with greater clinical significance because of the audience for which this book is intended. For example, we have chosen to describe high scores on Factor Q3 as representing the "ability to bind anxiety" rather than by the adjectives "compulsive, socially precise" which Cattell uses.

FACTOR A (Warmth)

Low Score		*High Score*
RESERVED, A—	versus	WARM, A+
(Reserved, Detached, Critical, Aloof, Stiff)		**(Warmhearted, Outgoing, Easygoing, Participating)**

Critical	vs.	Good Natured, Easygoing
Stands by His Own Ideas	vs.	Ready to Cooperate, Likes to Participate
Cool, Aloof	vs.	Attentive to People
Precise, Objective	vs.	Softhearted, Casual
Distrustful, Skeptical	vs.	Trustful
Rigid	vs.	Adaptable, Careless, "Goes Along"
Cold	vs.	Warmhearted
Prone to Sulk	vs.	Laughs Readily

A review of the items which measure Factor A is worthwhile. According to these items, if you like living in a sociable suburb, being a waiter versus a carpenter, if you have been elected to many offices, and would accept an invitation to be a worker in a charity drive, you would be a warm, helpful sort of person compared with someone who answered the alternatives in the other direction. Cattell (1957) notes that people high on Factor A are probably "easygoing, adaptable (in habits), warmhearted, attentive to people, frank, emotional, expressive, trustful, impulsive, generous, and cooperative." Evidently, a high-A person would be easy to have as a friend. People with low scores on A are said by Cattell to be "obstructive, cantankerous, inflexible, rigid, cool, indifferent, close-mouthed, secretive, anxious, reserved, suspicious, close, cautious, hostile, egotistical, impersonal, dry, and impassive"—apparently not such a pleasant person to have as a friend.

With regard to the clinical implications of scale A, it is noteworthy that in his early writings Cattell, following Kretschmer, felt that this factor corresponded to the classical distinction between schizophrenia and manic-depressive psychosis, as well as the milder variations of these mood swings in less disturbed persons. Consequently, he initially titled the factor "cyclothymia-vs.-schizothymia," making the implication evident. This initial titling of the factor should not be forgotten by those using the 16 PF clinically, for it may have much truth to it. However, it soon became apparent to those using the test that the terms were too extreme, and in the recent 16 PF *Handbook* Cattell and his co-authors refer to the factor as "sizothymia-vs.-affectothymia," thereby reducing the pathological associations of the identifications. Even more recently, in his 1973 book, Cattell has further shortened the term to "affectia-vs.-sizia."

"Sizothymia" is derived from the Latin word for flatness, and is meant to imply somewhat flattened affect. The meaning of "affectothymia" should present few problems for clinicians, for it is a direct reference to the affective psychoses. Thus, someone high on Factor A may be considered to be emotionally labile, while someone low on this factor probably demonstrates little affect. As examples, singer Pearl Bailey exemplifies A+ to her audiences, while actress Greta Garbo's admonition, "I want to be alone," seems to be characteristic of the A— person. To quote Cattell et al. (1970), "Social workers have to adapt cheerfully and flexibly to a lot of compromises with human failings, and to accept a ceaseless impact of never entirely soluble emotional problems that might drive the exact logician or the careful electrician mad." Social workers are known to be high on Factor A and electricians low (A—).

Addressing the question of psychopathology directly, someone who shows extreme deviations at either the A— or A+ end of the scale is likely to have troublesome traits. It is probably deemed preferable in our American culture to be high on A rather than low. There are people who make their way in life through the exercise of high-A tendencies almost exclusively. They are likely to be unhappy in jobs such as physicist or bookkeeper that require isolation from people. Should you notice that the person who is A+ is also very low on Q_2 (i.e., who is group dependent), the combination of the two factors would suggest that this individual might well be unhappy in solitary work, since the high group dependency would reinforce the need to exchange affect with other people. High A's can turn out to be very demanding in their interpersonal relations, since they frequently require much time and attention from others in order to gratify their own intense dependency needs.

On the other hand, someone with a very low score on A, a person who is extremely reserved and detached, might well be facing far more serious adjustment problems than the A+ person. A mild degree of introversion, such as a sten of 4, would suggest merely that the person was reserved or somewhat lacking in warmth. But should we find that the person is unusually low (i.e., a sten of 2 or even 1) on A, the probability of this score's representing only a mild personality disposition becomes less and less. In such an instance, the question would have to be asked as to why this person should avoid people so completely. After all, most people are generally aware that it is part of society's ideal to be warm and outgoing, yet the very low-A person is blatantly indicating that he prefers to be away from people.

It is quite possible for someone to be emotionally healthy and still obtain a low score on A. Famous researchers tend to have low A's. However, a low A should be checked into further in any case by examining the person's score on C (ego strength) or the second-order anxiety factor. In our experience, the odds of a low A occurring in combination with a high C are slim.

It could be expected that someone turning away from others to the degree that A— implies would probably have a history of unsatisfactory relationships with people. After all, something must have made him withdraw. It is further reasonable to hypothesize that the person probably obtained his detached outlook on life from his earliest interactions with others. This is, in extreme form, a description of the classic "burnt-child" reaction, wherein the person has come so to fear others as a result of highly unrewarding and austere family relationships in his early years that he avoids human contact. Thus, when a clinician encounters a patient with a score of 1 or 2 on the A scale, it is essential to determine through other means whether or not a severe problem does exist in this area of functioning. It would be naive to expect a scale of only 20 items to predict such trends with perfect accuracy, but the scale has sufficient accuracy to warrant a clinician's probing further if an extremely low A is obtained. Occasionally, one encounters a formerly high-A person who has been "turned off" by perceived rejection by others who had formerly played an important role in his life, and who has become A—. However, such changes may not be frequent; according to Cattell (1973), scale A has a substantial hereditary component.

Scale A is a prominent member of two of the second-order factors (see Chapter 5). The first of these is the introversion-vs.-extraversion factor (invia-vs.-exvia in Cattellian terminology). This second-order factor subsumes high scores on A (warmth), F (impulsivity), and H (boldness), and low scores on Q_2 (self-sufficiency). Scale A also appears on another second-order factor, tough poise (cortertia), along with I (emotional sensitivity) and M (imagination). We shall go more deeply into descriptions of these second-order factors later, but keep in mind that you should expect to find someone high on A also to be F+, H+, and Q_2—. If you find that someone doesn't fit this pattern, it is wise to try to discover why.

FACTOR B (Intelligence)

Intelligence, though not technically a personality trait in Cattell's view, was included in the 16 PF because of its importance in understanding many aspects of human functioning. This fact has been demonstrated by several pertinent studies (see Cattell, 1957). Scale B is the only scale on the 16 PF that doesn't follow the 0,1,2 or 2,1,0 scoring pattern. Only one answer is correct, and each adds only one point to the total score on the scale. Moreover, these items are hard! In the general population, only 2.3% of the people get 12 or more right out of the 13 items on Form A.

FACTOR B (Intelligence)

Low Score		*High Score*
LOW INTELLIGENCE, B—	versus	HIGH INTELLIGENCE, B+
(Dull)		**(Bright)**

Low General Mental Capacity	vs.	High General Mental Capacity
Unable to Handle Abstract Problems	vs.	Insightful, Fast-Learning, Intellectually Adaptable
Apt to Be Less Well Organized	vs.	Inclined to Have More Intellectual Interests
Poorer Judgment	vs.	Showing Better Judgment
Of Lower Morale	vs.	Of Higher Morale
Quitting	vs.	Persevering

Keep in mind that on the 16 PF a person's intelligence is converted to standard scores with reference to his or her particular normative group. Thus, a person getting 10 items correct would obtain a standard score of 8 in the general population, but a standard score of only 7 with respect to college students (male, Form A norms). This is obviously different from the usual practice followed on intelligence tests, where an I.Q. has essentially the same meaning in all groups. Consequently, a college student who obtained a standard score of, say, 6 on scale B would not be presumed to have an I.Q. of slightly above 100, but perhaps slightly above 115, or whatever one considers the average intelligence of college students to be. Should you like a comparison with the general population, however, that can be gotten simply by looking up the score in the general population norm tables.

The decision to place such a short, and hence probably somewhat inaccurate, intelligence scale on the 16 PF was made because the test authors thought it a good idea to give a complete picture of the whole person, and that of course must include intelligence. If, as is recommended by the test authors, you give all five forms (A through E) of the 16 PF to a patient, you could probably take the score as seriously as you would most of the major intelligence tests. Unfortunately, though, it is likely that most clinicians will continue to give only Form A of the 16 PF under the press of time, even though there is an appreciable benefit in increased reliability to be gained by giving Forms A and B.

Scale B has proved, in the authors' experience, to be valuable in spite of its shortcomings as an overall intelligence measure (Karson & Pool, 1957). If nothing else, it is a good indicator of the attention that the test taker has paid to the test. Should you find that any college student, for example, gets a chance number of items right on this scale (raw score of about 4), it is likely that the student has not read the instructions, or has become disinterested in the test half-way through the period of administration. Another interpretation might be that the student was trying to make a bad impression for some reason, perhaps to avoid a job that he doesn't want.

If you find a very low score, and yet there is evidence that the person was really trying to do well, further inquiry is warranted. Patients in the middle of an acute anxiety attack are apt to find it impossible to concentrate to the extent necessary to answer the questions on scale B. Assume that you find that a patient has obtained a low score on intelligence, and yet you are reasonably sure that he has been working hard on the test, as shown by the time taken to complete it. One procedure would be simply to ask him why he had so much difficulty with the intelligence items. These items seem to have an inherent fascination for persons taking the 16 PF; people who have completed the test ask more questions about these items than about the others. It is noteworthy that these scale B items are reported by many subjects to be among the most objectionable of all the 16 PF items. Consequently, it's likely that a person would remember some of the items, and he might well tell you something to the effect that he just couldn't concentrate on them. At the same time, some people simply haven't the motivation to spend the time necessary to figure out these tricky power items. Such an attitude toward the test is, in itself, worthy of study. It could reflect upon the sincerity of answering on the test as a whole. This could be further checked by looking at the Motivational Distortion or Random scale.

Scale B is also useful in reaching conclusions about implications raised by other scales. For example, were you to find that a person gets a sten of 10 on scale M (imagination), you might hypothesize that he is a really creative person, but you wouldn't want to make a statement to that effect unless you knew that he had the necessary intelligence to carry out his creative efforts. Similarly, should you suspect from a high score on scale N that a person was shrewd and worldly, you would again need information about his intelligence to tell how well he carries off his schemes. With high shrewdness and low intelligence, one would suspect that he might try to appear clever, but fail in the attempt; moreover, he might not be aware of his failure, as in the case of an inept psychopath.

Scale B, then, is frequently useful in making discriminations needed in the interpretation of the other personality factors, but a definitive conclusion would necessitate knowledge of the person's I.Q. from a good individual intelligence test, such as the Wechsler.

FACTOR C (Ego Strength)

Low Score		*High Score*
EMOTIONAL INSTABIL- ITY or EGO WEAKNESS, C—	versus	HIGHER EGO STRENGTH, C+
(Affected by Feelings, Emotionally Less Stable, Easily Upset, Changeable)		**(Emotionally Stable, Mature, Faces Reality, Calm)**
Gets Emotional when Frustrated	vs.	Emotionally Mature
Changeable in Attitudes and Interests	vs.	Stable, Constant in Interests
Easily Perturbed	vs.	Calm
Evasive of Responsibilities, Tending to Give Up	vs.	Does Not Let Emotional Needs Obscure Realities of a Situation, Adjusts to Facts
Worrying	vs.	Unruffled
Gets into Fights and Problem Situations	vs.	Shows Restraint in Avoiding Difficulties

One might well expect to find the concept of ego strength early in the list of factors, and so it does, on the third scale, C. A glance at the items on this scale makes it apparent that the C factor is measuring something much like ego strength, or lack of neuroticism. Someone low on C says that he lacks energy, has unreasonable fears, has trouble sleeping, and shows a certain resentment of others which is probably unreasonable. Amy March of *Little Women* comes to mind here as illustrative of low C.

Scale C and the second-order anxiety factor generally are among the most important indicators for the clinician searching for psychopathology. A person with low ego strength may be expected to have difficulty in adjusting to life on many fronts, and one can tell this by noting the rather broad area of problems covered by the scale C items. C is one of the best estimators of emotional stability among the first-order factors, and a low score here should serve as a warning signal to any clinician using the 16 PF. This is doubly so because many of the items on the scale are obvious, and hence easily fakeable. Almost everyone knows that he should have sufficient energy to face his difficulties (to paraphrase a Form A item), and that it isn't socially acceptable to have strong resentments. Consequently, if one finds a low score on scale C, one may infer one of two things: (1) the person may be faking bad, as many patients do who are seeking to get into psychotherapy, in the "hello" half of the "hello-goodbye" effect, or (2) the person is really in serious trouble, not being able to see the social implications of the items that he is answering. He might, for example, feel resentment toward other people, and yet not be aware how frequently and with what intensity he was expressing feelings of that nature. Situation two is generally more serious than the first one, but whatever the reason for a very low score on C, it should be very thoroughly investigated. Differentiation between the two situations can be made by inspecting the other scales. A person trying to look bad with the goal of seeking treatment in mind could be expected to have very high scores on O (guilt proneness), and Q4 (free-floating anxiety). A person simply unable to tell the difference between socially acceptable and unacceptable items might well have a high score on the more obviously pathological scales such as L (suspiciousness), and a very low score on Q3 (ability to bind anxiety). In short, although Factor C may signal difficulties in ego control, one will have to look for the specifics of the problem elsewhere. In any case, serious problems may be anticipated in the person's personality. The degree to which they may be modified is another matter.

Cattell (1957) notes that a person high on C may be considered "emotionally stable, free of neurotic symptoms, not hypochondriacal, realistic about life, unworried, steadfast, self-controlled, calm, patient, persevering and thorough, loyal, and dependable." One *low* on C is "emotional, dissatisfied, showing a variety of neurotic symptoms, hypochondriacal, plaintive, evasive, immature, autistic, worrying, anxious, changeable, excitable, impatient, quitting, careless, undependable morally." He sums it up by saying that a high-C person has the "capacity to express available emotional energy along integrated as opposed to impulsive channels," thus indicating that the personality fabric is holding together well. Cattell feels that this factor deals with the ability to express impulses well at a given time, rather than making a conclusion about the ability to plan one's whole life adequately. As an example of high C, the stalwart Mrs. Miniver comes readily to mind.

The implications of the factor for success in psychotherapy should be obvious. Someone with average or above average ego strength, whatever the indications from the other scales of the 16 PF, is likely to be a good candidate for psychotherapy. Should he be especially low on C, one should have reservations about the prospects for successful treatment, unless a more thorough examination tempers this hypothesis.

A survey of the content analysis of the senior author's blind analyses of the 16 PF demonstrates the "go-no-go" nature of this scale's utility. Virtually all of the comments made about C— profiles remarked simply on low ego strength and emotional instability. The comments about the C+ profiles dealt simply with the patient's possessing adequate ego strength, and the likelihood of successful psychotherapy.

Scale C varies together with H— (shyness), L+ (suspiciousness), O+ (guilt proneness), Q3— (inability to bind anxiety), and Q4+ (free-floating anxiety), on the second-order anxiety factor, on which scale C has one of the highest loadings (about .80). Consequently, one may expect scores on these scales to go up and down together. Variations in the pattern mentioned are useful in specifying the particular problems involved. Scale C is pretty much the same thing that Eysenck (1970) talks about when he discusses "general neuroticism," although this concept may be more closely allied to the entire second-order anxiety factor. This factor will be discussed subsequently in greater detail.

In brief, a low score on C invariably warrants further examination of the patient, while a high score is seen as indicating potential for improved adjustment (assuming Motivational Distortion is low). Among highly educated and sophisticated people, it is unusual to find a very low C, even though they may be presenting themselves for treatment. With persons of different cultural backgrounds, for example, adolescents not of the White-Anglo-Saxon-Protestant variety, a low score on C may not be quite so serious and may be indicative of something different, but it should always be checked out. On occasion, a high C is earned by a person with severe psychopathology, but it is usually, though not inevitably, accompanied by a high MD score. In any event, experience suggests that the high C in such a case be regarded with great skepticism. Instances like this have led us to interpret low-C scores with a good deal more confidence than high ones.

FACTOR E (Dominance)

Low Score		*High Score*
SUBMISSIVENESS, E—	versus	DOMINANCE OR ASCENDANCE, E+
(Obedient, Mild, Easily Led, Docile, Accommodating)		**(Assertive, Aggressive, Competitive, Stubborn)**
Submissive	vs.	Assertive
Dependent	vs.	Independent-minded
Considerate, Diplomatic	vs.	Stern, Hostile
Expressive	vs.	Solemn
Conventional, Conforming	vs.	Unconventional, Rebellious
Easily Upset by Authority	vs.	Headstrong
Humble	vs.	Admiration Demanding

The items on scale E clearly describe someone who enjoys dominating and controlling others as well as criticizing them (E+). Such a person likes being in command, enjoys meeting challenges, feels superior to others, and does not mind forcing his ideas on other people. Indeed, he enjoys it. Factor B (intelligence) is always important in interpreting E, since in many cases it determines what form the dominance will take. In our culture, low-B people are not too often permitted the luxury of dominance. During the latency period as well as in adolescence, peer groups and siblings often serve to extinguish high E when intelligence is not also high. On the other hand, it is interesting to attempt to resolve the contradiction when one encounters a high-B profile, accompanied by a low E. Perhaps body build variables also play a role here, or a dominating parent, or both.

The concept behind Factor E is very close to the common language usage of the term "dominance." Cattell (1957) feels that someone high on E will be "self-assertive, confident, boastful, conceited, aggressive, pugnacious, extra-punitive, vigorous, forceful, willful, egotistical, rather solemn or unhappy, adventurous, insensitive to social approval, unconventional, and reserved." As an example of E+, Lucy van Pelt from the comic strip "Peanuts" comes to mind. Cattell feels that someone low on E will be "submissive, unsure, modest, retiring, complaisant, impunitive, intropunitive, meek, quiet, obedient, lighthearted, cheerful, timid, retiring, tactful, conventional, frank, and expressive."[2]

E+ may not be as important in the determination of direct pathology as some of the other scales. It seems to be more useful in determining character traits such as chronic anger. In this connection, it is frequently valuable in evaluating sociopaths, as shown in the detailed example in Chapter 2. One can look for more pathology, however, in the case of low-E individuals. People who are excessively shy, humble, and accommodating may be suffering from a very painful degree of submissiveness, and E— might well have the same implications as were found with A— (aloof) individuals. In particular, when both E and A are extremely low, one could well expect that there must have been some early influences in the person's life which caused him to be afraid of

---

[2]Meg March, from Louisa May Alcott's *Little Women*, seems to fit this description of E— nicely.

people, even to the extent of developing schizoid tendencies, or the "burnt-child" reaction. It simply isn't wise to be too submissive in our society, in spite of the Bible's comments about the virtues of being meek. Should you find, then, that someone is low on A and E, a further inquiry into the person's ability to cope with hostility is warranted. For it is likely that every individual should, and does, feel a great deal of hostility. But an A— and E— person is strongly denying the hostility inevitably felt, and one should try to find out why. Should you also find that such a meek person were very low on F (impulsivity) and Q_1 (criticalness), and high on O (guilt-proneness) and Q_4 (free-floating anxiety), the possibility of suicidal tendencies could well be raised, since the hostility would appear to be turned almost totally back on the self.

The relationship of the E factor to the other factors is somewhat different with males than it is with females. In both, E+ is found along with L+, M+, Q_1+, and Q_2+ on the fourth second-order factor, independence. Thus, someone who is high on E (dominance) may be expected to show a high degree of suspiciousness (L+), imagination (M+), rebelliousness (Q_1+), and self-sufficiency (Q_2+). However, in the case of males, Cattell finds E on the second-order factor of extraversion, along with A, F, H, and Q_2—. This implies that a certain amount of dominant aggressiveness is found in males of our culture, and that it is not expected to be found in females to that degree. This difference agrees well with past roles of males and females in our society, based on cultural expectations.

Also relevant is the idea that if other hostile factors are present in a woman's profile (such as L+ or Q_1+), one could have the classic example of the "castrating" female. Extreme dominance and aggressiveness might imply that a woman was rebelling against her conservative female role stereotype. In marital counseling, should you find a male partner low on E, while his wife scored high on E, it would not be difficult to make a guess about who dominates in the family, especially if the wife is also higher on B (intelligence), N (shrewdness), and Q_1 (rebelliousness). Such a comparative pattern would not bode well for the marriage, although the wife might find it to her liking. Should the male partner become more dominant in such a marriage, say through psychotherapy, it is likely that the marital situation would deteriorate. At the same time, it is recognized that there are marriages of this sort that survive because they satisfy the sado-masochistic needs of the partners.

FACTOR F (Impulsivity)

Low Score		*High Score*
SERIOUSNESS, F—	versus	IMPULSIVITY, F+
(Sober, Taciturn, Serious)		**(Enthusiastic, Heedless, Happy-go-lucky)**

Silent, Introspective	vs.	Talkative
Full of Cares	vs.	Cheerful
Concerned, Reflective	vs.	Happy-go-lucky
Incommunicative, Sticks to Inner Values	vs.	Frank, Expressive, Reflects the Group
Slow, Cautious	vs.	Quick and Alert

With the introduction of scale F, we begin to run into difficulty in differentiating between the factors. If you compare the actual items on the scales, you may notice that the underlying concept of scale F is similar to that of scale A (warmth). This is largely due to Cattell's method of factor analysis, which allows factors to be related, but there still is a decided difference between the two scales. While scale A concerns itself with how warm and outgoing a person is, someone high on F, in contrast, is impulsive, flighty, unrestrained, and feels that he has a number of friends. But you won't necessarily find the helpful quality in an F+ that you would in an A+. Thus, a person who is F+ can be expected to have certain extraverted trends, but they are essentially self-centered in quality. Thus, if you had two flat tires on a lonely country road, you'd probably be a lot better off having an A+ person pass by than an F+ person. The A+ person is more likely to be helpful, while the F+ person would stop only if it suited his momentary whim.

Cattell (1957) associates the following adjectives with the high end of F: "cheerful, joyous, sociable, responsive, energetic, rapid in movement, humorous, witty, talkative, placid, content, resourceful, original, adaptable, showing equanimity, trustful, sympathetic, open." Those associated with F— are "depressed, pessimistic, seclusive, retiring, subdued, languid, dull, phlegmatic, taciturn, introspective, worrying, anxious, unable to relax, obsessional, slow to accept a situation, bound by habit, rigid, unstable in mood level, suspicious, brooding, narrow."

Scale F comes as close as anything on the 16 PF to measuring the clinical concept of manic-depressive tendencies. Although Cattell et al. (1970) warn that "desurgency (F—) should not be confused with depression," it has been the authors' experience that a low score on F coupled with a high O (guilt proneness) should not be ignored, and that F— frequently points in the direction of depression. From the items in the scale it should be obvious that someone who has the low opinion of himself indicated (few friends, dislike of social situations, lack of enthusiasm), certainly does not have much optimism about his future. As a result, a low F should be taken seriously, and looked into further, especially if other scales on the 16 PF point to problems with aggression, anxiety, and guilt. If you find a patient who is E— (submissive), F— (serious), O+ (guilt prone), and Q4+ (anxious), you should take the possibility of serious depression, perhaps even suicidal tendencies, into account. In all, you can expect that an F— person is responsible, sober, and serious in his approach to life. The image of a person no longer young in spirit emerges with F—, while at the high end, the picture of a happy-go-lucky adolescent comes to mind. Perhaps the early movie roles of Mickey Rooney in the Andy Hardy series exemplify F+.

It should be noted that F tends to be higher in younger persons, especially adolescents; a steep downward trend is found on this factor between the ages of 20 and 30. By 30, the person's personality should have stabilized. Consequently, the occurrence of a high F would not be unexpected in high school or college students, but it would be much rarer to find it in a 40-year-old man. For example, in the male college student norms, Form A, the mean score on scale F is 16.44 (raw score), while for the general population, 10 years older, the mean F is 14.17. This is a substantial difference, which makes our point neatly.

A high score on the second-order extraversion factor finds F+ (impulsivity) associated with A+ (warmth),

H+ (boldness), and Q2— (self-sufficiency). Indeed, in males, F has the highest loading on this factor (.84), but it shows no appreciable relationship to the other second-order factors at all. There is an interesting theory behind F+, presented by Cattell (1957), to the effect that F+ represents a lower experience of threat, punishment, and inhibition in early life, so that a high-F person is less susceptible to the intimidations of others in his environment.

Thus, F details the seriousness with which a person looks at life. If you were looking for a reliable, dependable, prudent person for an important job, you'd want a somewhat F— person (not too much so!). You might hire someone moderately high on F+ for a job, if he were rather young, in the expectation that he would "grow out" of his impulsivity and immaturity, especially if he were also high on C and Q3. If you need someone with a good deal of enthusiasm for a job, perhaps as a salesman, you'd look for high F. However, you'd have to watch out for the irresponsibility which frequently accompanies high F, especially if H (boldness) is also high and Q3 (compulsivity) is low.

FACTOR G (Group Conformity)

Low Score		*High Score*
LOW SUPEREGO STRENGTH or LACK OF ACCEPTANCE OF GROUP MORAL STANDARDS, G—	versus	SUPEREGO STRENGTH or CHARACTER, G+
(Disregards Rules, Expedient)		**(Conscientious, Persistent, Moralistic, Staid)**
Quitting, Fickle	vs.	Persevering, Determined
Frivolous	vs.	Responsible
Self-indulgent	vs.	Emotionally Disciplined
Slack, Indolent	vs.	Consistently Ordered
Undependable	vs.	Conscientious, Dominated by Sense of Duty
Disregards Obligations to People	vs.	Concerned about Moral Standards and Rules

The resemblance of the items on scale G to those on the MMPI "Lie" scale should be immediately apparent for anyone familiar with the Multiphasic. Scale G consists of a number of questions about what are considered ideal virtues in American culture. Anyone answering the questions so as to obtain the maximum score would be something of a stick-in-the-mud. It is unlikely that any real person would invariably acquiesce that sloppiness was disgusting, that the law was more important than occasional freedom, that he is never careless, that he always plans ahead, never admits to having a closed mind, and is strict, conscientious, and governed by strict rules (all examples of items). This is the "philistine" pattern on scale G that Cattell (1957) so nicely notices. Anyone who is strongly G+ could be considered an extremely moral, conventional, rigid person. Moreover, it should be rare to find very high scores among people who are not trying to distort their scores, unless they are professional moralists of some sort (ministers, rabbis, or priests), who for some reason feel it necessary to accept perfectionistic moral standards without question.

At the same time, it is worth checking a very low score on this scale. An extremely low level of moral awareness may be even more troublesome than an extremely high level. A very G— person might give little thought to helping others settle arguments, might thrive on disorder and sloppiness, and in general would show little concern for the standards of society. An extreme G— profile, thus, could indicate a serious lack of internal standards, and hence trends toward sociopathy. The seriousness of the trends would depend on whether "acting-out" behavior occurs. The probability of such an occurrence can frequently be judged from the other 16 PF factors, including extraversion, F (impulsivity), H (boldness), O (guilt-proneness), and Q_3 (ability to bind anxiety).

We should explicitly state here that the present writers disagree with Professor Cattell about the interpretation of the G scale. We prefer to deemphasize the superego aspects of Factor G, and, instead, believe that someone high on G may make a show of the external trappings of conventionality and morality without necessarily having achieved introjection of parental and societal standards, as in the case of sociopaths (see Chapter 2 in this regard).

49

Factor G, in our opinion, does not measure the guilt that someone feels about his actions, since there are no items that query the person about breaking the rules. To assess this aspect, the clinician would have to look further down the list of factors to scale O (guilt-proneness), as well as other indicators. We think it perfectly possible for someone to be very low on group conformity, but not feel any guilt about it. This would be the pattern of G— and O—, so often found in people with sociopathic trends.

A combination of scores frequently found on the 16 PF is that of a low G coupled with a high O. Here we have someone who would have us believe that he disregards the standards of society, but the intense guilt to which he admits belies this interpretation. Such a person is attempting to prove to himself that he has no internalized standards, but his strong guilt feelings contradict this argument. He knows the rules of the game, all right, but he's trying to circumvent them and suffers greatly from guilt at his lack of conformity. Such a pattern is common in adolescents, who often rebel against their parents' standards, but who nevertheless feel guilt over the conflict. Consulting rooms of therapists are filled by such people. The problem for the therapist will be that of trying to hold up a mirror to the patient so that he can see what he is doing in his relationships. Hopefully, he might then change the stimulus situation and thus break the vicious circle of nonconforming behavior followed by overwhelming guilt. Clinical experience suggests that Factor G is more easily modified or ameliorated than O; the latter seems to be extremely resistant to change.

Cattell (1957) provides the following descriptive adjectives for low G: "quitting, fickle, frivolous, immature, relaxed, indolent, unscrupulous, neglectful of social chores, changeable." High G's, on the other hand, are "persevering, determined, responsible, insistently ordered, conscientious, attentive to people, and emotionally stable." Queen Victoria of England comes to mind as an example of G+.

It should be clear from our previous discussion that too little or too much group conformity coupled with poor impulse control often leads to behavioral difficulties. Surprisingly, G is related to only one other factor on the 16 PF in a substantial way, and that is Q3 (ability to bind anxiety or compulsivity). These two scales go together to make up the second-order factor of sociopathy which we shall describe when we consider the second-order factors in detail.

In summary, we find that scale G measures the degree to which a person has been conditioned to conform to the ideals of his group, and how well he understands the rules of the social game which we all must play. A low score on scale G does not imply that the person feels guilty about his lack of group conformity; this aspect must be assessed through scale O (guilt proneness).

FACTOR H (Boldness)

Low Score	*High Score*
SHYNESS, H—	BOLDNESS, H+
(Shy, Timid, Restrained, Threat-sensitive) versus	**(Adventurous, "Thick-Skinned," Socially Bold)**
Shy, Withdrawn vs.	Adventurous, Likes Meeting People
Retiring in Face of Opposite Sex vs.	Active, Overt Interest in Opposite Sex
Emotionally Cautious vs.	Responsive, Genial
Apt to Be Embittered vs.	Friendly
Restrained, Rule-bound vs.	Impulsive
Restricted Interests vs	Emotional and Artistic Interests
Careful, Considerate, Quick to See Dangers vs.	Carefree, Does Not See Danger Signals

If you look up the items on scale H, you'll find that this factor is one of daring venturesomeness, spontaneity, and summing it up best of all, risk-taking. We have accordingly nicknamed it the "Errol Flynn" factor. H embodies all Errol Flynn stood for in the movies, namely, a willingness to accept any challenge, an adventurous and roving nature, and high overt interest in the opposite sex.

Differentiation of H+ from A+ and F+ is at first difficult. However, if you look at the items in the descriptions of the other two scales, you'll find that there is a "talkative, witty, limelighting, light, 'Gallic' quality to F that is not found in H+" (Cattell, 1957). F+ implies a certain narcissism and less caring about the feelings of others than does H+. At the same time, you can differentiate A+ from H+ by noticing that there is a good deal more boldness in H+. But these three factors are nonetheless highly related, as shown by the correlation (in males) of .44 between A and H, and of .66 between F and H.

The low-scoring end of H (H—) may well be of more interest to the clinician studying pathology than the H+ end, which is more indicative of a character trait. This may be seen in the fact that in earlier writings Cattell referred to this trait as "withdrawn schizothymia-vs.-adventurous cyclothymia." Thus, both A— and H— were at one time thought to be associated with schizoid tendencies, H— being the more strongly associated of the two. Even in 1957, Cattell still stated that "the H— pole so *strongly* suggests 'schizothyme withdrawal,'" and in the recent 16 PF *Handbook,* H— is referred to as "the temperament which, in stress, shows proneness to schizoid disorders . . . ." Since A— and H— are both indicative of somewhat the same thing,[3] should you see a profile with very low scores on both A and H, the hypothesis of tendencies toward withdrawal should be made. The particular kind of schizoid withdrawal can be assessed by looking at the other scales of the 16 PF. For example, should you find someone with A—, H—, but with a strong tendency toward suspiciousness (L+), the possibility of paranoid trends should be considered.

Cattell (1957) finds the following adjectives associated with the H— pole of the factor: "shy, timid, withdrawn, little interest in the opposite sex, aloof, cold, self-contained, hard, hostile, secretive, inhibited, conscientious, recoils from life, lacking confidence, careful, and considerate." H+'s, on the other hand, are "adventurous, like meeting people, show strong interest in the opposite sex, gregarious, genial, responsive, kindly, friendly, frank, impulsive (but no inner tension), like to 'get in the swim,' self-confident,

---

[3]The fact that A and H are strongly correlated is due to the fact that Cattell allows his factors to be related. See Chapter 5, on second-order factors.

and carefree.'' Beth March from *Little Women* comes readily to mind as an example of H—, while her sister, Jo, is clearly H+.

The comment made about the adjective ''impulsive (but no inner tension)'' points out the difference between H+ and E+ (dominance). The high-E person is driven to be dominant, but the H+ person is simply bold and gregarious by nature, and his dominance (which is certainly there) is of a much nicer quality than that of the E+ person. The E+ person is ruthless in the pursuit of what he seeks, while the H+ person would be more diplomatic about getting what he wants.

In 1957, Cattell felt that there were strong hereditary components in H+, although he has tempered this view somewhat in his 1973 book. Coupled with this, and by implication, there are strong physical, particularly autonomic determinants to this factor. He says (1957), ''The H+ person is one in which the normal parasympathetic predominance is not easily shaken by the sympathetic system (threat) or other interrupting responses.'' That is, the activation of the sympathetic nervous system is well controlled. The opposite is true of the H— person, who has strong reactions to threat, or is threat-sensitive; hence the term ''threctia,'' which Cattell prefers to use as the basic descriptive term for the H— end of the factor. Errol Flynn, in his movies, was dauntless in his actions, and by no means sensitive to threat (H—); on the contrary, he actively sought out challenges, as did James Bond. You have to be a bit of an Errol Flynn to be a success in our society, and it should be obvious that if you're too threat sensitive, you'll probably miss taking a few risks that you should. If you don't take any risks, you won't get anywhere (''nothing ventured . . .''), and if you don't get anywhere, you're going to be frustrated and your hostility is apt to present even more of a threat to you, to which you'll be increasingly sensitive, and another vicious circle is begun.

Factor H is associated with two of the second-order factors, namely, extraversion (A+, F+, H+, and Q_2—) in both males and females, and the second-order anxiety factor (C—, H—, L+, O+, Q_3—, and Q_4+). From this association with both the extraversion and the anxiety factor, we may infer much of what has already been discussed, namely that H+ is primarily a characterological matter (boldness or venture-someness) and H— is indicative more of pathology (great threat sensitivity, timidity, and schizoid shyness).

In short, if you're high on H, there is a good chance that you will like to travel, take a lot of risks (but probably with planning), have many good friends, be convivial, and, in short, enjoy practically everything that makes life worth living. If you're H—, you won't. Need we say more? Oh, yes. H+ persons seem to be more prone to high blood pressure and coronary infarcts. So perhaps there is a price to pay in terms of longevity after all.

FACTOR I (Emotional Sensitivity)

Low Score	*High Score*
TOUGH-MINDEDNESS, versus I—	EMOTIONAL SENSITIVITY, I+
(Tough-minded, Rejects Illusions)	**(Tender-minded, Sensitive, Dependent, Overprotected)**
Unsentimental, Expects Little	vs. Fidgety, Expecting Affection and Attention
Self-reliant, Taking Responsibility	vs. Clinging, Insecure, Seeking Help and Sympathy
Hard (to point of cynicism)	vs. Kindly, Gentle, Indulgent to Self and Others
Few Artistic Responses (but not Lacking in Taste)	vs. Artistically Fastidious, Affected, Theatrical
Unaffected by "Fancies"	vs. Imaginative in Inner Life and in Conversation
Acts on Practical, Logical Evidence	vs. Acts on Sensitive Intuition
Keeps to the Point	vs. Attention-seeking, Flighty
Does not Dwell on Physical Disabilities	vs. Hypochondriacal, Anxious about Self

We recommend that you look up the items on this factor, as we have for all previous factors. Scanning these items, you'll find that there are at least two general trends to be found in the factor: (1) a love of cultural things, and (2) a dislike of meddling in situations involving hostility. In many ways Factor I is similar to the Mf scale on the MMPI; indeed it correlates .54 with it. The similarity to the Mf scale is not in Mf's original interpretation as an indicator of homosexuality, but instead with regard to its later implications as to the level of one's cultural interests (Karson & Pool, 1957).

You should be aware, by the way, that we are now getting into factors which are contributing less and less variance or information to our study of personality. Remember that the factors on the 16 PF are ordered in the amount of variance or importance which they carry. However, even factors of lesser variance on the 16 PF, and especially Factor I, can be of great usefulness in the description of personality.

Cattell (1957) lists the following adjectives as descriptive of I—: "emotionally mature, independent-minded, hard, lacking artistic feeling, unaffected by 'fancies,' practical, logical, self-sufficient, responsible, free from hypochondria." Those associated with I+ are: "demanding, impatient, dependent, immature, kindly, gentle, aesthetically fastidious, introspective, imaginative, gregarious, attention-seeking, frivolous, and hypochondriacal."

This factor is clearly what William James had in mind when he made his famous distinction between "tender-minded" and "tough-minded" persons (see Cattell, 1946), although Factor M (imagination), which correlates highly with I, also has something of this flavor to it. The present authors have accordingly nicknamed this factor for Humphrey Bogart, at the low pole, and for Leslie Howard, at the high pole. If you prefer female examples, Mae West would be I—, and Dora Copperfield from Dickens' novel, I+.

Clinically speaking, Factor I is not closely associated with pathology, especially if it is the only deviant score on the profile. One can anticipate that someone with a very low score on I probably is repressing the components of his personality which involve emotional expression, but this is not necessarily pathological unless expression of emotions is required in his life. Thus, someone who is very low on I, and hence very tough-minded, would probably be uncomfortable in the helping professions, such as psychiatric social work or clinical psychology. Even this is not clear-cut, though, for we have seen many social workers who were quite tough-minded.

Such people often have great success in working with clients who are E— (dependent) and I+ (emotionally sensitive), and who apparently need strongly directive psychotherapy.

At the other end of the continuum, putting a sensitive, I+, tender-minded person into a position as an industry tycoon would be a mistake. However, it is unlikely that such an error could occur. The characteristics indicative of either end of the dimension are sufficiently evident both to the person and those evaluating him that a sort of natural selection would usually prevent improper placement.

From the standpoint of the ability to endure stress, it may be better to be I— than I+, at least in the case of Air Force airmen. Should you be too emotionally sensitive and find life in the military too harsh, as does the I+ person, you could very well develop psychosomatic complaints under stress. However, even among air traffic controllers, who are distinctly less emotionally sensitive (I—) than the general population, psychosomatic symptoms are not unknown. We conclude therefore that, if put under enough continuous stress, both I+ and I— persons could and do develop symptoms.

Although it is likely that the I+ person would succumb sooner, at least in an all-male environment, it is important to emphasize that the personality profile, taken in its entirety, cannot be disregarded in such instances. For example, in 1959 Karson reported a total of seven significant differences between psychosomatic problem cases and a well-adjusted group of Air Force airmen, not only on Factor I, but on Factors A, B, C, O, Q_2, and Q_4 as well. Factor I also turned out to be the most significant discriminator of all the factors when samples of boys with conduct problems were compared with boys with personality problems (Karson, 1965). It is such results as these that suggest why I is such a fascinating personality variable, even though it is not as large in variance as those described earlier in this chapter.

FACTOR L (Suspiciousness)

On the basis of simple face validity, it is clear that Factor L is one of the most indicative of disturbance of all the 16 PF scales. Someone obtaining a high score on L insists on getting his point across, feels that people are talking about

FACTOR L (Suspiciousness)

Low Score		*High Score*
TRUST, L—	versus	SUSPICIOUSNESS, L+
(Trusting, Accepting Conditions)		**(Suspecting, Jealous)**

Accepts Personal Unimportance	vs.	Jealous
Pliant to Changes	vs.	Dogmatic
Unsuspecting of Hostility	vs.	Suspicious of Interference
Ready to Forget Difficulties	vs.	Dwelling upon Frustrations
Understanding and Permissive, Tolerant	vs.	Tyrannical
Lax over Correcting People	vs.	Demands People Accept Responsibility over Errors
Conciliatory	vs.	Irritable

him behind his back, cannot endure human frailties, is oppositional, likely to fight, antagonistic and quick to take offense, to paraphrase some of the items. This is clearly the common psychiatric syndrome of paranoia, if carried to the extreme. Cattell refers to a high score on L as "protension," which is short for "paranoid-trend." In their automated report-writing system (Karson & O'Dell, 1975), the authors frequently refer to this dimension as "anxious insecurity." This identification adds another aspect to the meaning of the factor, and should be apparent from the item content.

Cattell (1957) lists the following adjectives as characteristic of low-L people: "trustful, understanding, composed, socially at home." High-L people are described as "suspicious, jealous, self-sufficient, withdrawn." These lists are rather short, since we are now down to the ninth factor, which has a good deal less information contained in it than the first few.

It should be obvious that someone with a high score on scale L is probably going to be difficult to get along with, although we have already noted that people with high scores on scale E are similarly not pleasant to be around. But the reasons are different, for the person with a high score on E (dominance) is merely controlling and aggressive; it may be that there is a good reason for the aggression. With the L+ person, the reasons for the aggression are probably not well rooted in reality. The L+ patient is resentful and hostile, a person who typically projects and displaces angry feelings. The reason may perhaps go back to his childhood, to a time when difficult interpersonal relationships with the nuclear family led to a deep-seated mistrust and resentment of other people, stemming from continually frustrated dependency needs.

Thus, a high score on L almost certainly is worth looking into, especially in view of the fact that most people should be aware of the fact that L+ answers are not socially desirable. Anyone taking the 16 PF should be aware that it is not a good thing in our society to admit to oppositional trends, to feelings of reference, and to making trouble just for the fun of it (all paraphrases of items). The very fact that someone is so pushed by his inner impulses that he is unable to keep the ideals of society in mind should be taken seriously. Thus, while it is not conclusive evidence of pathology to discover a high score on L, again, it warrants further inquiry.

The opposite end of this dimension, L—, must be regarded as a healthy sign, even if extreme. Someone with a sten of only 1 or 2 on L may be altogether too trusting and adaptable to a fault. But such an attitude is often refreshing in our society. True, this person might frequently be disappointed by others, but apparently it does not result in a great deal of resentment in the L— person. Someone very low on L might well be considered a "nice guy," and even if his childish trust leads to disappointment, he usually gets over it.

Scale L keeps company with a number of other factors on the second-order anxiety factor, along with C— (low ego strength), H— (shyness), O+ (guilt proneness), Q3— (inability to bind anxiety), and Q4 (free-floating anxiety). Since this second-order factor is the best single indicator of conflict on the 16 PF, and since L+ is one of several important contributors to this factor, the implication that it should be considered as evidence of disturbance is reinforced.

Cattell (1957) does not feel that L+ automatically implies paranoia, in view of the fact that many scientific researchers and clever attorneys have been found to have high L. Further, Factor L did not correlate significantly with the MMPI Paranoia scale in pilots, although it did with 10

other MMPI scores (Karson, 1958). Previous work hints that
L+ could measure anxiety and rigidity, rather than paranoid
suspicion as originally believed (Karson & Pool, 1958).

FACTOR M (Imagination)

Low Score		*High Score*
PRACTICALITY, M—	versus	IMAGINATION, M+
(Practical, Has "Down-to-Earth" Concerns)		**(Imaginative, Bohemian, Absent-minded)**
Conventional, Alert to Practical Needs	vs.	Unconventional, Absorbed in Ideas
Concerned with Immediate Interests and Issues	vs.	Interested in Art, Theory, Basic Beliefs
Prosaic, Avoids Anything Far-fetched	vs.	Imaginatively Enthralled by Inner Creations
Guided by Objective Realities, Dependable in Practical Judgment	vs.	Fanciful, Easily Seduced from Practical Judgment
Earnest, Concerned or Worried but Steady	vs.	Generally Enthused, but Occasional Hysterical Swings of "Giving Up"

With the 10th factor we are getting to scales
which contribute smaller amounts of variance. This is shown
by the fact that one encounters some difficulty in gaining a
clear-cut pattern of the meaning of the scale from the items
(look them up), or even from the adjectives which Cattell listed
in 1957. At that time, he felt that M— persons were "conventional, uninterested in art, practical and logical, conscientious,
worrying, anxious, alert, poised, had tough control and
narrower interests." M+ persons were described as "unconventional, eccentric, esthetically fastidious, sensitively
imaginative, 'a law to himself,' undependable, placid, complacent, absorbed, with occasional hysterical emotional upsets
and intellectual, cultural interests."

An immediate conclusion from both the items
of the scale and the adjectives just given is that M+ indicates
intellectual, aesthetic pursuits, while M— indicates the lack of

such interests and perhaps the active denial of them. Someone who is M— is generally intensely practical, while someone who is M+ is generally indifferent to, although not necessarily unaware of, practical matters. M+ people can be absent-minded at times and quite unconventional or Bohemian. M+ also implies a good deal of fantasy life, which has led us to dub it the "Walter Mitty" factor, after James Thurber's famous character. It may well be that M+ is the best single indicator of potential creativity on the 16 PF, especially if it can be established that the person in question does in fact have high intelligence (B+).

M— people, on the other hand, are thoroughly practical persons,[4] similar to the "tough-minded" persons found as I—. That I and M are closely related may be seen from the fact that they are found together on the second-order factor of tough poise or cortertia. As with the other 16 PF primary factors, but perhaps even more so with M, one has to look at the context in which a deviant score on Factor M occurs. For example, M+ associated with B+ (intelligence) in a person with Q3+ (compulsivity) will be quite different from M+, B+, and Q3—. In the former case, there is some control on the fantasy activity with much potential for channeling the creative effort. In the latter case, it is much more likely that the fantasy activity is dissipated and rarely, if ever, comes to fruition, whether in art, music, research, or literature.

The work that an individual performs is crucial in making a proper determination of whether it's good to be high or low on this factor. The authors have never had a really capable secretary who was M+, regardless of the rest of the 16 PF profile. One such secretary was very pleasant, but could rarely be counted on to attend to important details. In discussing her 16 PF profile with her, she told us that her husband seldom permitted her to do the grocery shopping, for

---

[4]Perhaps the practicality of the M— individual can best be illustrated by the following story. The meaning of life has been a perennial question since the dawn of man. One man, after having married and raised a family as well as running a successful business, became obsessed with this question. He haunted libraries, traveled widely, neglected his family and business, and consulted experts all over the world. Twenty years passed in his search for the meaning of life, but all to no avail. Finally, he was told about a certain Rabbi who might be able to give him the answer he sought, if anyone could. He straightaway went to consult the Rabbi. The great moment arrived when the seeker, by now an old bedraggled and unkempt man with a peculiar intensity about him, accosted the Rabbi and demanded to know the meaning of life. "Well, my son," explained the Rabbi, "life is like a fountain——." The utterance so enraged the seeker that he rudely interrupted and shrieked: "You mean that I've deserted my family, ruined my business, lost my health, and wasted my life, to hear you tell me that life is like a fountain?" Whereupon the Rabbi shrugged, stretched his arms out sideways, and replied: "So, it's not like a fountain . . . ."

she would invariably forget certain major items which her spouse would then have to pick up. Incidentally, she was also E+ (dominant).

In air traffic control work, a job which requires close attention to detail, workers with M+ profiles are a distinct rarity (Karson & O'Dell, 1974). It should be apparent that in such work M+ is clearly a liability. However, in other occupations, M+ would not necessarily be a handicap. M— was one of three primary factors which significantly discriminated anxiety neurotics from psychosomatic cases (Karson, 1959), with the latter group having a lower mean score on M. Factors M and I are both significantly related to Hs on the MMPI, but not to D or Hy (Karson & Pool, 1957).

FACTOR N (Shrewdness)

Low Score		*High Score*
NAIVETE, N—	versus	SHREWDNESS, N+
(Forthright, Unpretentious)		**(Astute, Worldly)**
Genuine, but Socially Clumsy	vs.	Polished, Socially Aware
Has Vague and Injudicious Mind	vs.	Has Exact, Calculating Mind
Gregarious, Gets Warmly, Emotionally Involved	vs.	Emotionally Detached and Disciplined
Spontaneous, Natural	vs.	Artful
Has Simple Tastes	vs.	Esthetically Fastidious
Lacking Self-insight	vs.	Insightful Regarding Self
Unskilled in Analyzing Motives	vs.	Insightful Regarding Others
Content with What Comes	vs.	Ambitious, Possibly Insecure
Has Blind Trust in Human Nature	vs.	Smart, "Cuts Corners"

If you look up the items on scale N, you'll see that a person high on N admits to playing his cards rather close to his chest, isn't interested in physical activity, places a premium on being with polite people, has little interest in the outdoors, is more interested in retaining calm in a group than getting his opinions across, and in general seems to know how to use people and manage groups to get things done without creating a fuss. This scale, then, seems to measure the socially important personality trait of poise or sophistication, or, as it is called on the 16 PF profile sheets, "shrewd, calculating, and worldly." N correlates significantly only with the Hysteria scale on the MMPI ($r = .25$), and it shares little in common with other 16 PF factors as well. Its highest correlation is with E (dominance), where $r = -.40$.

Factor N may be an important dimension in predicting future occupational success in demanding, careful work, such as in air traffic control. In this sample of people, N resides on a second-order factor with G (group conformity) and Q_3 (ability to bind anxiety or compulsivity).

The context in which N occurs is important in its interpretation. Someone with N+ accompanied by B+ (intelligence) and Q_1+ (rebelliousness) could surely be troublesome to his supervisors by manipulating others, especially if this N+ person were also E+ (dominant).

Cattell (1957) lists the following adjectives as being descriptive of N—: "socially clumsy, awkward, vague and sentimental mind, company-seeking, lacking independence of taste, lacking self-insight, and naive." N+ is described as "polished, socially skillful, exact mind, cool, aloof, esthetically fastidious, insightful regarding self, and insightful regarding others."

Thus, someone low on N is likely to be inept in social relationships, while the N+ person is able to keep sufficient distance from others to have the potential to get along very well in the world. We say "have the potential" because N+ in itself does not mean that the person would necessarily put his abilities into action. One would expect a confidence man (the logical extension of the idea of N+) to have a high score also on dominance (E+), and on boldness (H+).

Similarly, it should be apparent that someone must be sufficiently high on intelligence to present a good social front, and hence get along well in the world. It is therefore important to look at scale B before making a definite statement about a person's effectiveness in this regard.

A few quotes from the writers' content analysis may serve to further clarify the interpretation of this factor:

Sten Score on Scale N	Comment
1	He is also seen as a somewhat naive individual who has had little experience in groups, since he tends to be altogether too forthright and direct. This implies a certain childishness about him ....
4	... somewhat clumsy in social relations ....
9	... his high score of 9 on N suggests a shrewd and calculating individual ....

All things considered, we have found scale N somewhat less useful and reliable than the other scales. But there have been occasions when it has proved to be an invaluable addition to the 16 PF.

FACTOR O (Guilt Proneness)

Low Score	*High Score*
UNTROUBLED ADEQUACY, O—	versus GUILT PRONENESS, O+
(Self-assured, Placid, Secure, Complacent)	**(Apprehensive, Self-reproaching, Insecure, Worrying, Troubled)**
Self-confident vs.	Worrying, Anxious
Cheerful, Resilient vs.	Depressed, Cries Easily
Impenitent, Placid vs.	Easily Touched, Overcome by Moods
Expedient, Insensitive to People's Approval or Disapproval vs.	Strong Sense of Obligation, Sensitive to People's Approval and Disapproval
Does Not Care vs.	Scrupulous, Fussy
Rudely Vigorous vs.	Hypochondriacal and Inadequate
No Fears vs.	Phobic Symptoms
Given to Simple Action vs.	Lonely, Brooding

Although scale O is considered by Cattell (1957) to be the least adequately defined of all the factors derived through the English language analysis, nonetheless our experience has shown this to be one of the two most important scales on the 16 PF from a clinical standpoint. A glance at the items shows again and again the worrisome anxiousness and guilt that is associated with many clinical syndromes, especially obsessional worrying. Feelings of vague dread, guilt for no reason at all, extreme reaction to criticism, fear of criticism and punishment, and poor self-esteem, are the bread and butter of many therapists.

The adjectives listed by Cattell (1957) as descriptive of this factor show roughly the same thing. O— adjectives include "self-confident, self-sufficient, accepting, tough, and spirited." O+ adjectives are "worrying, lonely, suspicious, sensitive, and discouraged."

Clinical experience with this scale has shown that scores other than the average signal disturbance all too frequently. That is, *either* O— or O+ scores bear investigation. If one is too untroubled, the question is immediately raised as to the adequacy of superego controls. On the other hand, if the person admits to excessive worries, then the problem of overwhelming guilt is raised. Here Lady Macbeth comes to mind as an illustration of O+ .

As mentioned under scale G, there is an interesting relationship between G (group conformity) and scale O (guilt proneness) which merits repetition. It should be apparent to anyone familiar with Freudian theory that both of these concepts refer in some way to the superego, and in our experience the relationship goes this way: Someone high on G may safely be assumed to be aware of the standards of society, but the question of how well the superego standards have been introjected can be answered only by the elevation of scale O. One frequently encounters situations in which a person scores high on O and hence is subject to intense feelings of guilt. But at the same time he is very low on G, implying low conformity to group standards. Such a person is caught in a vicious circle of neurotic conflict. But, unlike someone who is O—, he pays very heavily for his infractions as a result of his overly severe, archaic, superego-generated guilt feelings. This pattern is particularly important in certain adolescents, who frequently rebel against parental and societal values.

The importance of this scale, from a clinical standpoint, may be seen in the fact that it is one of the most important contributors to the second-order anxiety factor, which consists of C— (low ego strength), H— (shyness), L+ (suspiciousness), O+ (guilt proneness), Q3— (ability to bind anxiety), and Q4+ (free-floating anxiety). As mentioned before, anxiety is the most important single factor in the determination of psychopathology, and O is tied for second place in importance on this factor in both male and female groups. Moreover, a simple reading of the items would suggest immediately that someone high on O would be under a good deal of tension, and hence neurotic. This factor proved to be the best discriminator on the 16 PF when a sample of mothers of emotionally disturbed children was compared with a control sample (Karson, 1960).

It has been our experience that, in addition to simple apprehensiveness, O+ may be a good indicator of depression, especially if the other trends important in depression are present on the profile. Thus, if you should run across a person who is O+, and who at the same time shows a good deal of exaggerated seriousness (F—), you'd be wise to look into the pattern. We have observed that O+ may sometimes be a response to a recent traumatic event in a person's life; for example, it could arise from the suicide of a spouse, or the death of a parent. Given such traumatic circumstances, O may fluctuate more than the other anxiety indicators, and thus may be highly subject to situational influences which one ordinarily attributes to state rather than trait measures of personality (Cattell & Scheier, 1961).

Unfortunately, it has been our experience that the guilt behind O+ is very difficult to extinguish even after intensive individual or group psychotherapy (Karson & Wiedershine, 1961). When a therapist encounters an O+ patient, it is often tactically more profitable to concentrate one's efforts at raising G, rather than lowering O. That is, getting the patient to realize that the price paid for his unconventional behavior is simply not worth the subsequent painful guilt feelings aroused, and thus breaking the neurotic entrapment.

THE "Q" SCALES

The scales contained in the remainder of this chapter (those based on Q-data, or questionnaire data) have been found only in questionnaires to this point. As a pure researcher, Cattell feels that these scales, not having been found in all forms of data, are less firmly established than scales A through O. Thus, they have been put at the end of the 16 PF profile sheet, with the "Q" designation, to indicate their special status. The reader interested in pursuing these subtle distinctions is referred to Cattell's writings, especially the enormous compendium that he wrote with Warburton (1967), *Objective Personality and Motivation Tests.*

The present writers find these "Q" scales to be invaluable. Scale Q_4, in particular, is to us the best single indicator of anxiety on the 16 PF. At the present state of development of the art, if you wish to find out about someone's subjective experience of anxiety, you simply have to ask him about it through a questionnaire. Behavior ratings are more or less useless for this purpose at the present time.

Even though the "Q" scales are found at the end of the profile sheet, then, the clinican will be well advised to give them a prominent place in the integration of a case. In reading through the cases at the back of the book, you will find that the "Q" scales are used as frequently, if not more so, than any of the other scales.

FACTOR Q_1 (Rebelliousness)

Low Score		*High Score*
CONSERVATISM OF TEMPERAMENT, Q_1-	versus	RADICALISM, Q_1+
(Conservative, Respecting Established Ideas, Tolerant of Traditional Difficulties)		**(Experimenting, Liberal, Analytical, Free-thinking)**

If you look up the items on scale Q_1, you'll note that they imply a strong desire to overturn current customs. Q_1 bears a good deal of resemblance to Factor E (dominance) in the face validity of the items. However, there is less emphasis on dominance and hostility in Q_1, and more on constructive reforms. Nevertheless, it seems reasonable to assume that a Q_1+ person would not have many compunctions about trampling someone who got in the way of his reforms. In 1957, Cattell listed no adjectives to help explain this factor, but instead gave sample questionnaire items, the substance of which was the following:

(*a*) an opinion that societal difficulties arise from ignorance and lack of scientific ideas about life, rather than from a lack of goodwill and religious ideals; (*b*) admission of a preference for books by H. G. Wells, rather than historical movies; (*c*) a preference for chess (a hostile, competitive game, if you've ever played it) over croquet; (*d*) an admission that one is occasionally afraid of his ideas because they are so unreal; (*e*) a feeling that one learns more in school by reading textbooks rather than going to class; and (*f*) a preference for reading about social issues in the modern world rather than local news in the papers.

Again, these imply a radical, experimenting approach to life, and the great concern with social issues that seems to typify modern times.

Clinically, although Q_1 is probably more descriptive of a character trait than anything else, it should be apparent that it is not an unwarranted assumption that an extreme Q_1+ person probably has an unresolved Oedipal conflict. The high-Q_1 person probably has not learned to handle his problems with authority figures well. Consequently, the writers refer to the Q_1+ person as having a "Fidel Castro" complex, in honor of the Cuban revolutionary. You may substitute your favorite political radical for Castro, if you like. As a female counterpart, Emma Goldman, the American anarchist from Russia, is a good example.

It should be apparent that the Q_1+ person is probably not going to make a very staunch subordinate in a work setting. One can assume that such a person may get into difficulty when he interacts with authority figures. Furthermore, you can be pretty sure that he is going to look for a scrap. This is not to say that high-Q_1 persons are not useful, especially if you're planning to tumble down the walls of Jericho or some other politically offensive establishment. But since most people are of necessity followers rather than leaders, and since high-Q_1 persons are typically not happy followers, Q_1+'s can be disruptive in a company setting. Indeed, if you should find that a person is high on Q_1, and at the same time is high on E (dominance) as well as L (suspiciousness), it is obvious that he would be hard to get along with. If he is B+ (intelligent) as well, you might be well advised to expect his attacks on an intellectual plane. In women, high critical and castrating tendencies have been observed as correlates of Q_1+, especially when accompanied by B+ (intelligence) and H+ (boldness). Dissatisfaction may also develop in women of this sort whose husbands are H— (shy) or E— (submissive) (Karson & Haupt, 1968).

Q_1 keeps company with E+ (dominance), L+ (suspiciousness), M+ (imagination), and Q_2+ (self-sufficiency) on the second-order factor of independence. We shall go into this second-order factor later, but it should be apparent from the scales comprising it that a high score could prove irksome. Q_1 has its highest correlations with Hy and Mf in pilots (Karson & Pool, 1958).

It is interesting to note that Q_1 is not mere adolescent rebelliousness, but expresses itself in intellectualized forms of hostility. Scores on this scale are said to increase into middle life. After all, our culture teaches that direct aggression is not permitted, except in sports. In our society children are expected to express angry feelings through sublimation. However, since not everyone can be a Jim Brown or Muhammad Ali, intellectual channels for expressing hostility are also encouraged, such as bridge, editing of journals, cross-examination in courts of law, employment interviews, and the like. Thus, indirect expression of aggression (Q_1) is permitted, while direct expression is largely frowned upon.

Cattell et al. (1970) make the profound observation that "It has been said that the most conservative stage of man is in childhood." The high-Q_1 person can be a thinking radical rather than an activist, especially if he is also B+ (intelligent) and Q_3+ (compulsive). An excellent example of just such a person is George Bernard Shaw. At the same time, Q_1+ accompanied by poor impulse control and imbalance on the other scales, might well imply immature rebelliousness of a more reckless sort.

FACTOR Q2 (Self-Sufficiency)

Low Score		*High Score*
GROUP DEPENDENCY,	versus	SELF-SUFFICIENCY,
Q2—		Q2+
(Sociably Group Depend-ent, A "Joiner" and Sound Follower)		**(Self-sufficient, Resource-ful, Prefers Own Decisions)**

The items on this scale clearly indicate that this is a sort of introversion-extraversion factor. Some of the items that Cattell (1957) lists as descriptive only further this interpretation: A belief that there are more fools than nice people in the world, and a preference for finding out something about a social problem from a textbook rather than a recent novel on the topic. This is the kind of introversion that one would expect to find in scholars and scientists; that is, a relatively healthy, creative sort of introversion. As Cattell (1957) says, "The Q2 individual avoids society because it wastes time, not because of any emotional rejection, and because experience has told him his thinking is well enough organized to solve problems for himself." One can't resist quoting the *Handbook* on this scale: "Occupationally, Q2 is very high for executives, scientists—and criminals." Apparently, criminals share at least one trait in common with scientists (if not more)! However, the rest of the profile in which Q2 is embedded is apt to be very different.

This scale correlates significantly only with Si (Social Introversion) and Mf (Masculinity-Femininity) on the MMPI in pilots (Karson & Pool, 1958), and consequently is not related to the general maladjustment factor measured by the MMPI. However, deviations from the norm in either direction, especially in conjunction with other scale deviations, can have diagnostic significance. For example, should you find a person who is extremely high on Q2, and very low on all the other second-order extraversion factor scales, namely, A— (reservedness), F— (seriousness), and H— (shyness), you would begin thinking not so much in terms of good work habits or high self-sufficiency, but instead in terms of extreme withdrawal from people. This would be especially the case if intelligence (B) were low, indicating that the withdrawal was not a matter of intellectual choice. It is all very well to be self-sufficient, but such a pattern would indicate an almost complete turning away from other people.

At the same time, being too low on Q_2 (too group dependent), while not as serious as the situation just considered, can also have implications. A certain amount of self-sufficiency is necessary to function well in many activities in our society, and someone almost wholly without it, and at the same time inordinately high on F (impulsivity), is likely to have difficulty in certain jobs. A Q_2- person might well be influenced by bad company, and could get into trouble with the law, for example.

With regard to Q_2's membership on the second-order factors, we have already mentioned the presence of this scale on the second-order extraversion factor, made up of $A+$ (warmth), $F+$ (impulsivity), $H+$ (boldness), and Q_2- (self-sufficiency). However, Q_2 is also an important contributor to another second-order factor: independence. This factor subsumes $E+$ (dominance), $L+$ (suspiciousness), $M+$ (imagination), and Q_1+ (rebelliousness), as well as Q_2. All of these scales reflect independence and self-sufficiency, but in very different ways.

A final warning: Notice that the group dependence indicated by Q_2- is not the same thing as the group conformity suggested by $G+$. The correlation between the two is only about $-.15$. In other words, although one might expect a $G+$ person to also be low on Q_2, or, for that matter, for a low-G person to be Q_2+, the facts are that this simply isn't likely to happen. Q_2, further, is a major contributor to the second-order extraversion factor, while G is not.

FACTOR Q3 (Ability to Bind Anxiety)

Low Score		*High Score*
LACK OF CONTROL, Q_3-	versus	ABILITY TO BIND ANXIETY, Q_3+
(Uncontrolled, Lax, Follows Own Urges, Careless of Social Rules)		**(Controlled, Exacting Will Power, Socially Precise, Compulsive, Following Self-image)**

The items on this scale appear to measure something closely akin to self-control or a careful, calculated approach to life. A person who is Q3+ is programmed to think before he acts and to keep things in order. He does not let his emotions run away with him. This scale is somewhat similar to ego strength (Factor C) and conformity to group standards (Factor G), but it does not have the moral implications of G, and does not emphasize the ego-disorganization of C—. Obviously, someone high on Q3 is likely to possess good work habits, and is accustomed to keeping his emotions under control. A Q3+ person is someone who can effectively channel his energy. He can be depended on to be a good organizer and to get things done. He is typically a well-controlled, even compulsive person.

Thus, it is better for good mental health to be high on Q3 than it is to be low. Indeed, the writers believe that Q3 is usually an excellent indicator of how successfully a person is able to bind his anxiety. At the same time, too high a score on Q3, coupled with L+ (suspiciousness) and G+ (group conformity) can be indicative of undue obsessiveness and rigidity. Are there any negative consequences of being too high on Q3? Probably. Productive and creative people are often Q3+. But very high sten scores (8 or above) are unusual in such people. And our experience indicates that when anxiety is too tightly bound, creativity and flexibility may suffer. Certainly, the Q3+ person is not going to be tolerant of much ambiguity or disorder in his life, and disorder is often essential at some stage in the creative process. A Q3— person will often find it difficult to perform successfully in a large corporate or government hierarchy in which responsibility and compulsivity are rewarded. Should Q3— be coupled with the other anxiety indicators, it can safely be assumed that the person is in serious distress. Such a person would be unable to organize his impulse life so that he could put his energy to constructive use rather than dissipating it.

An obvious extrapolation from what has been said is the idea that someone who is high on Q3 will be happy and comfortable in his job and will have a well-defined occupational identity. If he were very Q3—, he might not remain in a job long enough to develop any identity at all! In fact, Q3— often suggests that insufficient identity has been developed in the person under consideration. This idea is similar to the concept of role diffusion put forward by Erikson (1950).

The flavor of Q3+ can be gotten from a paraphrase of the items listed by Cattell (1957). Someone high on Q3 is more energetic at getting his work done than other people, keeps trying when a problem is difficult to solve, sticks to it when faced with an obstacle, and never makes a promise that he can't keep.

As you might anticipate, Q3 is an important contributor to the second-order anxiety factor, along with C (ego strength), H (boldness), L (suspiciousness), O (guilt proneness), and Q4 (free-floating anxiety). But it is not as strong a component on this factor as the others. Generally, the clinician will find that Q3 is most useful as an indicator of ability to control emotions, particularly anger and anxiety. Indeed, Q3 proved to be one of the best discriminators on the 16 PF when a sample of mothers of disturbed children were compared with a matched sample of mothers of better adjusted children (Karson, 1960).

FACTOR Q4 (Free-Floating Anxiety)

Low Score	*High Score*
LOW TENSION, Q4— versus	HIGH TENSION, Q4+
(Relaxed, Tranquil, Torpid, Unfrustrated, Composed)	**(Tense, Frustrated, Driven, Overwrought, Fretful)**

The Q4 scale items are typical of what one would expect to find in an individual suffering from classic anxiety neurosis. The high-Q4+ person admits to tension, difficulty in calming down, inability to tolerate criticism, sleeplessness, concern about future happenings, an admission of not holding one's tongue at the proper times, and similar items. Q4 may well be the most important single indicator of acute neurotic trends on the 16 PF. Note that many of the items on Q4 are readily transparent, and hence easily faked. A high score usually implies that the person is under so much tension that he is overwhelmed by it. Apparently, at the moment of answering the questions, he cannot tear himself away from his problems for a sufficient length of time to give socially desirable answers, or else he subscribes to these items as a cry for help.

The transparency of the items suggests that Q4 can vary over time with the perceived state of the person taking the 16 PF. One day he may be so anxious that he answers almost all the questions in the "bad" direction, and another day he may have the anxiety temporarily under control, and make a much better showing. Since Q4 is easily fakeable, it is important, when encountering a low score, to inquire about the test-taking attitude of the examinee. In particular, should one find that *all* the anxiety indicators are in the low-anxious direction (i.e., L—, O—, Q4—, and C+), one should consult the Motivational Distortion scale described in Chapter 1. In such instances, thorough psychological and psychiatric interviews may be required to get at the facts of the matter. At times, low or average Q4 scores, along with low scores on the other anxiety scales, are found in patients with psychosomatic problems. Apparently, once the anxiety has been bound in a symptom, it is no longer consciously felt. Accordingly, it is not wise to conclude that a patient is healthy just from a knowledge of his Q4 score alone. One must not only know the person, but the characteristics of the particular sample from which he comes, as well as the base rates for the problem in question (Karson & Sells, 1956).

Factor Q4 successfully discriminated anxiety neurotics and those with somatic symptoms from a carefully matched group of well-adjusted Air Force enlisted men (Karson, 1959). It also discriminated a sample of fathers of boys with personality problems from those with conduct problems (Karson & Haupt, 1968), but not the mothers. However, it did discriminate a group of mothers of emotionally disturbed children from a control group of mothers of well-adjusted children (Karson, 1960).

Q4+ is the anxiety indicator par excellence on the 16 PF, among the first-order factors. It is also the most important contributor to the second-order anxiety factor. It has been our experience with many different age groups in a wide variety of clinical settings that one should always take a Q4+ score seriously. It is not wise to attempt to explain away this score on the basis of unusual circumstances. In such instances, it is a good idea for the clinician to review and discuss the individual items with the patient. We have encountered very few people with Q4+ in whom the free-floating anxiety was not apparent either immediately or later in the interview. Trembling and sweating are frequently manifested. On the other hand, we can recall cases where a person with a Q4— score appeared quite anxious in the interview. This merely demonstrates the ease with which the scale may be faked.

Factor Q4 correlated significantly with all of the MMPI scale scores except for Pa and Ma in a sample of Air Force pilots (Karson & Pool, 1957). In fact, the Pearson correlation between scores on Q4 and Pt was .75. No wonder we choose to describe Q4 as a measure of free-floating anxiety.

5

The Second-Order Factors of the 16 PF

One technical point must be mentioned to assist you in understanding the idea of second-order factors. When one conducts a factor analysis, one has the choice of coming up with factors which are related to one another, or with factors which are completely unrelated. There is a long-standing debate among experts who conduct factor analyses as to whether related or unrelated factors are best. Cattell believes that related factors allow one to obtain factors better aligned with reality (and we agree with him). It is infrequent to find things in the real world which are completely independent of one another. Thus, while manic-depressive psychosis and schizophrenia are usually thought of as completely separate (independent) disorders, they do have many symptoms in common. Schizophrenics often seem depressed, and depressives often show disorientation which is reminiscent of schizophrenia. If one tried to get the various diagnostic classifications by means of factor analysis, it would be difficult to obtain these two syndromes if relationships between factors were not allowed. There are good arguments for the use of unrelated ("orthogonal") factors in special circumstances. But Cattell has chosen to use correlated ("oblique") factors in the 16 PF, and so we won't discuss unrelated factors further.

If one has related factors, as in Cattell's system, it is then possible to conduct another factor analysis on the original factors. This process ends up with what are called "second-order" factors. In practice, with the 16 PF, this is done by giving the test and factor analyzing the correlations among the 16 scales. The resulting second-order factors are thought of as being much broader and more general in their scope than the primary factors, and they provide a useful way of summarizing the relationships found among the 16 PF scales. For example, the first of the second-order factors is broadly defined as introversion-vs.-extraversion, and includes A (warmth), F (impulsivity), H (boldness), and Q2— (group dependence). Intuitively, these things *do* go together. Take Bob Hope as an example of someone presumably high on extraversion. He's clearly outgoing (A+), makes a living at being enthusiastic (F+), ventures all around the world entertaining troops, at considerable risk (H+), and there's little doubt that he's dependent on the reactions of his audience to him (Q2—). The average correlation between the scales of this second-order factor is about .40. Obviously, they are related, but not perfectly, and the second-order factor extracts the dimension that they have in common. These second-order factors are the most suitable place for a novice to begin an initial perusal of a 16 PF profile. It is wise to take the second-order factors seriously when scanning a profile, especially the second-order anxiety factor.

There is one troublesome result of the decision to allow related factors. For example, since Factors A (warmth) and H (boldness) are allowed to be related, a purely mechanical approach to interpretation of a 16 PF profile can lead to difficulties. It is possible, on occasion, to find a person very high on A, but low on H. Possible, but unusual. A clinician making an interpretation directly from the first-order scales might conclude that the person is "warm, outgoing, greatly interested in participating with people" (A+), and in the next breath state that he is "shy, timid, and sensitive" (H—). This looks like a direct contradiction. One such discrepancy in a clinical report can totally destroy its credibility. A seasoned human interpreter will not make such errors. He can get around the problem through consideration of other pertinent elements in the profile in relation to the clinical knowledge he has garnered over the years. But a mechanical computer interpretation system, or a beginning clinician, may unwittingly make such a self-contradictory report. Note that if one followed Cattell's advice and used only new words for new concepts, there would be no contradiction between "affecto-thymia" (A+) and "threctia" (H—), thus showing the wisdom of that strategy.

Five major second-order factors in adults are usually found in the 16 PF, in addition to intelligence, which is found at both the first- and second-order levels. These are (I) extraversion, (II) anxiety, (III) cortertia, (IV) independence, and (V) sociopathy.[1] You will find others listed in various 16 PF references, but these are the main ones. Anxiety and extraversion are the two major second-order factors in the questionnaire realm. They have been shown repeatedly to account for the largest amount of information or variance in personality functioning. Much less is known of the nontest correlates of the others, so that we will emphasize the first two.

The easiest way to obtain second-order factor scores is simply to have the scoring done by a reputable scoring service, such as IPAT. If the clinician is strapped for time, there are worksheets available from IPAT that provide a simplified hand-calculation procedure for obtaining these scores.

Second-Order FACTOR I (Extraversion)

The first of the second-order factors is the well-known introversion-extraversion factor, identified by Jung many years ago. A person who scores high on extraversion is typically high on A (warmth), F (impulsivity), and H (boldness), and low on Q2 (self-sufficiency). Figure 5-1 demonstrates a profile answered in such a fashion as to obtain the maximum extraversion score; the clinician should become sensitized to such a profile, along with its converse, that for the minimum extraversion score.

Over the years, Cattell has varied somewhat in his consideration of which scales constitute this second-order factor. In the 16 PF *Handbook.* for example, we find that

---

[1] In his writings Cattell has identified this factor by its opposite pole and calls it "superego strength." This is how it is identified in the 16 PF *Handbook,* for example. Since it involves Factor Q3 as well as Factor G we have chosen to refer to it by the broader title of "sociopathy" in our writing.

FIGURE 5-1

16 PF PROFILE SHOWING MAXIMUM EXTRAVERSION

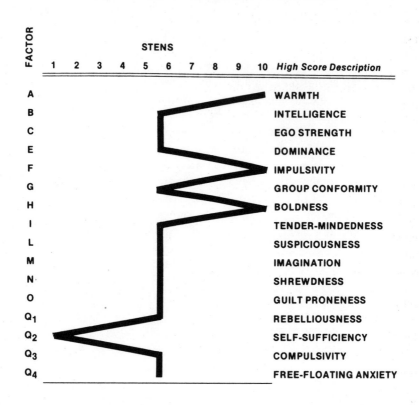

E+ (dominance) is included as part of this factor. However, in his most recent book on questionnaire factors (1973, p. 116), we find that E+ is not considered part of the factor. The present writers have long felt that E is not really part of this factor, at least in the groups that we have dealt with (Karson & O'Dell, 1974). At the same time, it is possible that E is of importance in certain groups; only a careful factoring in that group can resolve the question with certainty. In our discussion, we shall not consider E as part of the second-order extraversion factor.

Figure 5-1 may be a bit misleading, for there are many patterns of first-order factor scores which may lead to the same score on extraversion. Figure 5-2 shows a number of profiles, all of which result in an overall extraversion score of about 8. Notice that generally the pattern of scores is about the same, but at times there are great departures. Fortunately, most of the time A+, F+, H+, and Q2— tend to go together. But the clinician should be aware of the possibility of departures from the classic pattern.

We do not view extraversion as the principal factor pointing to emotional disturbance on the 16 PF. That role is reserved for the second-order anxiety factor. Nonetheless, extreme scores should be carefully considered in formulating a diagnostic report. The most pathologic of all the signs obtainable from extraversion occurs when a patient is encountered with an extreme tendency toward introversion. Such a profile, in its most exaggerated form, is plotted in Figure 5-3. Such a person is extremely reserved (A—), serious (F—), shy (H—), and very self-sufficient (Q2+). The pattern would only be compounded if the score on E (dominance) were also found to be very low, indicating submissiveness.

Introversion is not a bad trait, in moderation. For example, it is common for research scientists to be somewhat introverted. A researcher has little call to behave warmly (A+), would find it impractical to be impulsive (F+), or socially venturesome (H+), and generally has little need for frequent interaction with groups of people (Q2—). Even so, with most researchers, one does not usually find as radical a profile as that of Figure 5-3. Ordinarily, sten scores of 3 to 8 are the maximum deviation found in normal people, whatever their inclinations.

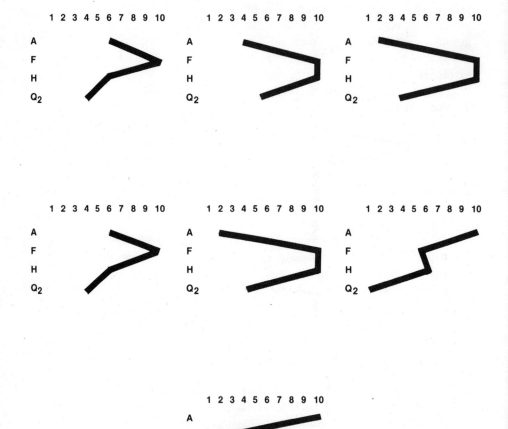

80

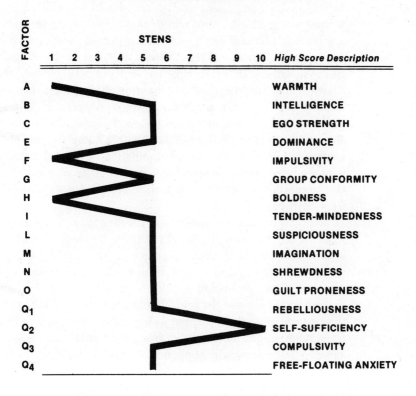

FIGURE 5-3
16 PF PROFILE SHOWING MINIMUM EXTRAVERSION

Consequently, should a clinician run across someone with scores of 1 or 2 on the second-order extraversion factor, or its component scales, he should immediately be alerted to the likelihood of withdrawal. There may be a very low level of libidinal energy in such a person. Someone with such extreme scores is likely to show the most severe tendencies associated with the various first-order factors, namely, the "burnt-child" reaction already mentioned with regard to extremely low A, the tendency toward depression and/or flattened affect associated with low F, and the schizoid shyness and withdrawal associated with a complete denial of venturesomeness (H—). This combination of scores, coupled with an avoidance of people implied by a score of 9 or 10 on Q_2, suggests a need to escape from other people which is not frequently encountered.

An interpretation given any extreme score must be tempered by the scores of the individual component scales. Thus, someone with an extraversion sten score of 2, say, might have gotten it by getting a score of 8 or so on H, very low scores on A and F, plus a high score on Q_2. This pattern would remove the schizoid element inherent in H from the pattern, and would present a very different picture indeed from what might be inferred from the extraversion score alone. The same would happen if A, say, were high, in the context of an extremely low extraversion score. Here, the possibility of the "burnt-child" reaction would be much lower than if A were not high. Whatever the cause, however, a very low score on extraversion should be taken seriously, for generally the scores do imply marked withdrawal.

A high score on extraversion is usually not as troublesome to a person's adjustment as a very low one. As with high A, a good deal of extraversion is frequently looked upon with favor in our society, and may be equated with a good deal of libido, in the positive sense of the term. However, if it is found that a person has an extraordinarily high score on extraversion, it may well be that something is amiss: too much need for interaction with others can be detrimental if one has to work in solitary settings. In other instances, the high extraversion score may mean that the person cannot subsist without continually demanding dependency gratification from others (low Q_2). It would be especially troublesome if a person high on extraversion also were E+ (dominant), B+ (intelligent), and Q_1+ (rebellious). Such a person would probably not only be very intelligent and critical, but would also be possessed of enough energy, impulsivity, and boldness to be difficult to get along with.

However, all in all it is likely that high scores on extraversion make for better adjustment in contemporary American life than do very low scores. Extraversion was found to be more amenable to change than anxiety in a military hospital setting on a sample of male and female psychiatric outpatients undergoing dynamically oriented group psychotherapy (Karson & Wiedershine, 1961).

Second-Order FACTOR II (Anxiety)

This second-order factor, in spite of the numbering system, often comes out to be of first importance among the second-order scales on the 16 PF. Study after study on the test has found the major primaries on this key factor to be (in order of importance), Q_4 (free-floating anxiety), O (guilt proneness), C (ego strength), L (suspiciousness), and Q_3 (ability to bind anxiety). This is true with all groups, of both sexes. At times Factor H (boldness) pops up on the factor, but not with sufficient regularity for us to include it as a major component.

Anxiety is the principal indicator of pathology on the 16 PF. A high second-order anxiety score should *always* be taken seriously. Should you see a profile like Figure 5-4, in which all of the anxiety scores are maximally elevated, a thorough psychological and psychiatric evaluation of the person in question may be indicated. A profile such as that found in Figure 5-4 is clearly a plea for help. This sort of plea may be at the unconscious level, in that the person making it may not be aware of it. Thus it is particularly important to look into the matter. Someone possessing little ego strength (C—), much paranoid suspiciousness (L+), great guilt (O+), an almost total inability to bind anxiety (Q_3—), and high free-floating anxiety (Q_4+) is in serious trouble. It is possible, of course, that a person with this sort of a pattern can merely be attempting to look bad for one reason or another. But the matter is of such grave interest that it cannot be ignored. It must be examined.

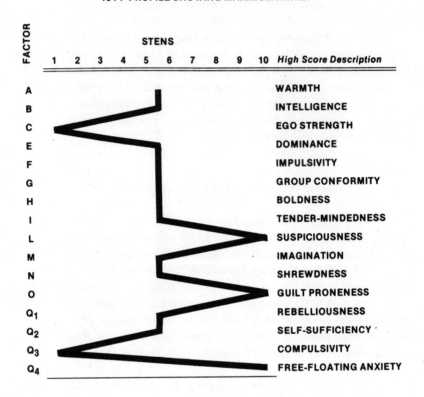

FIGURE 5-4
16 PF PROFILE SHOWING MAXIMUM ANXIETY

At the same time, a very low score on anxiety is not necessarily indicative of mental health. Figure 5-5 shows a profile with the lowest possible scores on the anxiety factors. Such a profile may of course indicate good ego integration. But at the same time, since the component primary factors of the anxiety factor are so easily faked (as seen in a previous chapter), a low score may mean only that the patient is trying hard to look good on the test. The MD scale, described in Appendix A, is invaluable for clearing up this point. A very low anxiety score, with a strongly elevated Motivation Distortion score, will mean quite another thing than would the same score with a low MD. The problem with a low anxiety profile, coupled with a high MD, is that we know that the person is hiding something, but we can't know precisely what. However, this very transparency of the anxiety factors makes it all the more important to take a high anxiety profile seriously. A person responding in such a manner is openly admitting to great distress, and consequently is usually aware of his plea for help.

Figure 5-6 shows a number of different patterns of factors that can lead to a second-order anxiety score of 8. The reader should study this figure until he has grasped the underlying pattern that distinguishes the anxiety syndrome. Fortunately, in spite of the multiplicity of patterns, one almost always finds that Q4 (free-floating anxiety) is elevated; this is generally an immediate signal that anxiety itself is likely to be high.

We have found over the years that the score on C (ego strength) strongly moderates the interpretation of anxiety. A person with a score of 7 on the second-order anxiety factor may have a C of, say, 2, or a C of 7. The person in the second case would have a relatively good prognosis in psychotherapy, since it would appear that his ego defense organization possesses the necessary resources to handle problems in a more constructive way. The person with the C of 2 would have a much poorer prognosis. Such low ego strength can be compared to a threadbare tire with many patches on it, the patches being the result of previous life stresses. As the tire rolls along, the patches loosen, and the air escapes, eventually causing a catastrophic malfunction. Someone with high ego strength, however, can handle stress much better.

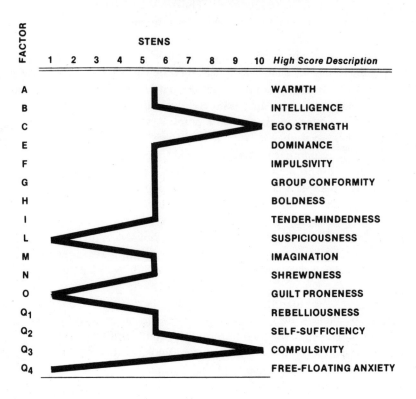

FIGURE 5-5
16 PF PROFILE SHOWING MINIMUM ANXIETY

FIGURE 5-6

VARIOUS PATTERNS OF PRIMARIES, ALL LEADING TO
AN ANXIETY SCORE OF APPROXIMATELY 8

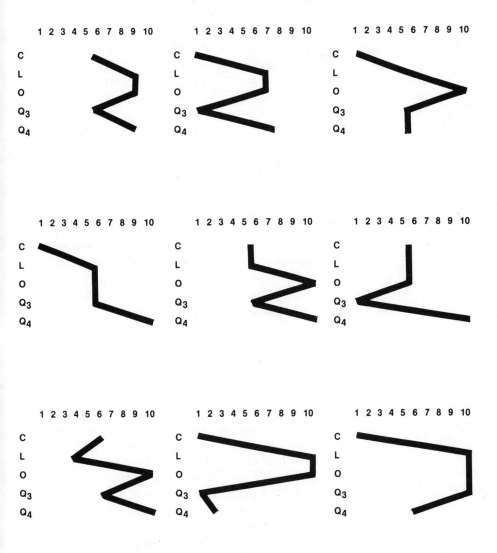

He may feel strong discomfort under stress, but the potential disintegration implied by low ego strength is not present.

Typically, when Q4 is high, Q3 is low, but not always. Occasionally one sees a profile where both Q4 and Q3 are high, leading one to conclude that the ego defense structure is extremely overtaxed. What seems to be required in that case is lessening the stress by removing the person from the intolerable situation he is confronting. We recall one case who earned the maximum on all the major 16 PF anxiety indicators. This young man's anxiety was so great that he would get up every few minutes to urinate. His anxiety was so contagious that even the therapist got the urge to go to the bathroom! When shown his 16 PF profile, this young man looked it over sadly, and said, "I know that, Doc. But what can I do about it?" Eventually he was taught to structure his life so that time would not hang so heavily on his hands. He later joined the military service, which provided him with the structure he needed to function adequately.

Unfortunately, in our experience, high anxiety is rarely that easily treatable. Often it proves extremely resistant to attempts to extinguish or ameliorate it (Karson & Wiedershine, 1961). From a diagnostic standpoint, anxiety has been demonstrated to be high in parents of child guidance patients and to be significantly higher in these parents than in a comparable sample of normal mothers (Karson, 1960). Unfortunately, it still appears to be true that it is far easier to diagnose anxiety than it is to treat it.

Second-Order FACTOR III (Tough Poise or Cortertia)

The clinical implications of the second-order factor of pathemia-vs.-cortertia (tough poise) are not thoroughly established as yet. However, the present writers have found it extremely useful in work with the sorts of occupational groups that we evaluate, especially in the case of air traffic controllers. Someone high on tough poise has *low* scores on A (warmth), I (emotional sensitivity), and M (imagination). Figure 5-7 shows a profile with an extremely high score on cortertia. People high on cortertia are aloof, tough-minded, and not prone to fantasy activity. Hence, we feel that such persons are much less likely to be swayed by their feelings than by their intellect. Air traffic controllers are lower on A, I,

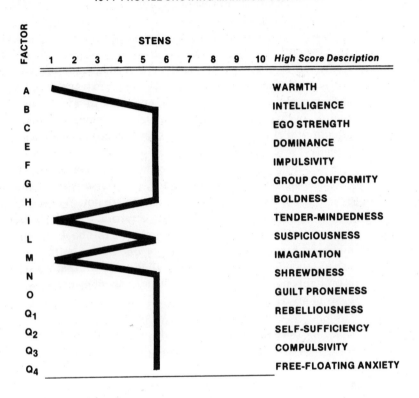

FIGURE 5-7

16 PF PROFILE SHOWING MAXIMUM CORTERTIA

FACTOR	STENS	High Score Description
	1 2 3 4 5 6 7 8 9 10	
A		WARMTH
B		INTELLIGENCE
C		EGO STRENGTH
E		DOMINANCE
F		IMPULSIVITY
G		GROUP CONFORMITY
H		BOLDNESS
I		TENDER-MINDEDNESS
L		SUSPICIOUSNESS
M		IMAGINATION
N		SHREWDNESS
O		GUILT PRONENESS
Q1		REBELLIOUSNESS
Q2		SELF-SUFFICIENCY
Q3		COMPULSIVITY
Q4		FREE-FLOATING ANXIETY

and M than are persons in the general population, and hence higher on cortertia (Karson & O'Dell, 1974). High cortertia has also been shown to be related to success as a pilot, another demanding occupation.

It is our position that persons *low* on cortertia (that is, with *high* scores on A, I, and M) are less likely to be controlled by their intellect and as a consequence are easily swayed by their feelings. It is an obvious extrapolation that such persons are a bad risk for positions in which careful control over one's feelings is essential, along with close attention to the job. Figure 5-8 shows a profile with an extremely low score on cortertia.

The term "cortertia" is a contraction for "cortical alertness." Tough-minded, cool persons are thought to be more mentally alert than those who are not. We shall use the terms "tough poise" and "cortertia" synonymously throughout the cases in the remainder of the book. Keep in mind, however, that cortertia is not one of the better established second-order factors on the 16 PF, and for that reason it is probably not wise to make conclusions about someone on the basis of his cortertia score alone.

Second-Order FACTOR IV (Independence)

The fourth second-order factor is called subduedness-vs.-independence. The primary factors which load it are E+ (dominance), L+ (suspiciousness), M+ (imagination), Q_1+ (rebelliousness), and Q_2+ (self-sufficiency). Figure 5-9 shows an extreme pattern of scores in the independent direction, and 5-10 shows the opposite, dependent pattern. Independence is not one of the better established 16 PF second-order factors. but it can be useful at times. Someone high on independence can be exceptionally difficult to get along with, as may be seen from the first-order factors that go to make it up. This is not altogether because of high hostility, but rather just because the person likes to do things in his own way. The *Handbook* suggests that someone high on this second-order factor is independent in the broadest sense, and is a person who is a "law unto himself."

We use independence only occasionally in our case writeups. But at times one runs across a pattern exactly like that of Figure 5-9, and then the concept is invaluable.

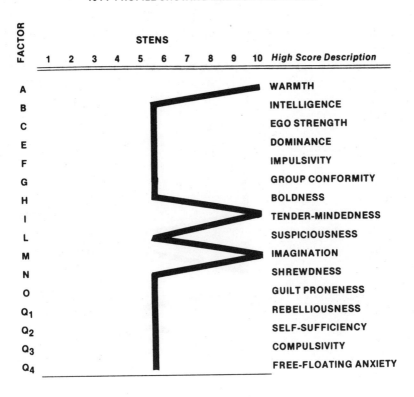

FIGURE 5-8
16 PF PROFILE SHOWING MINIMUM CORTERTIA

91

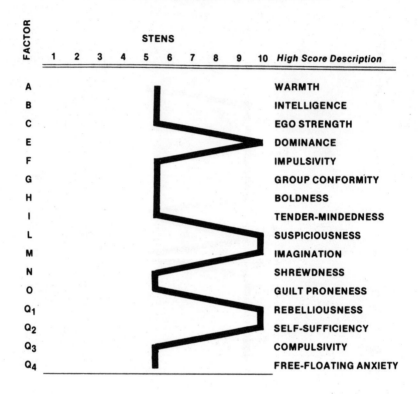

FIGURE 5-9

16 PF PROFILE SHOWING MAXIMUM INDEPENDENCE

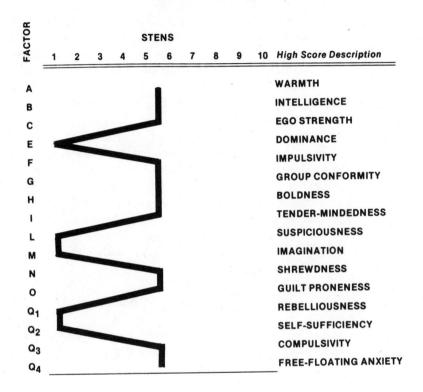

FIGURE 5-10

16 PF PROFILE SHOWING MINIMUM INDEPENDENCE

FACTOR	STENS	High Score Description
	1 2 3 4 5 6 7 8 9 10	
A		WARMTH
B		INTELLIGENCE
C		EGO STRENGTH
E		DOMINANCE
F		IMPULSIVITY
G		GROUP CONFORMITY
H		BOLDNESS
I		TENDER-MINDEDNESS
L		SUSPICIOUSNESS
M		IMAGINATION
N		SHREWDNESS
O		GUILT PRONENESS
Q_1		REBELLIOUSNESS
Q_2		SELF-SUFFICIENCY
Q_3		COMPULSIVITY
Q_4		FREE-FLOATING ANXIETY

Second-Order FACTOR V (Sociopathy)

This factor, called in full "compulsivity-vs.-sociopathy," was initially found in 1958 by Karson and Pool in a sample of Air Force pilots. It has been replicated on numerous occasions in samples of Air Force recruits (Karson, 1961), air traffic controllers (Karson & O'Dell, 1974), and in several other studies. Typically, G+ (group conformity) and Q3 (ability to bind anxiety) are the major primaries subsumed by this factor, although L (suspiciousness) and Q2 (self-sufficiency) are occasionally found on it also.[2] As we noted earlier, Cattell chooses to emphasize the positive character integration implied by G+ and Q3+, while the present writers opt to emphasize the negative aspects. We prefer to focus on the conformity, rigidity, and lack of spontaneity at one pole of the factor, as well as the freedom and lack of restraint at the other pole. Recent evidence suggests that prisoners do, indeed, score significantly different from controls in the expected direction.

The Remaining Second-Order Factors

In the 16 PF *Handbook,* and on the profile sheets of certain scoring services, you'll find other second-order factors mentioned. Generally, these have not been so well established by basic research and so we shall mention them only in passing. The 16 PF *Handbook* lists "naturalness-vs.-discreteness" and "cool realism-vs.-prodigal subjectivity," but even Cattell concedes that the "criterion associations have not yet been investigated" (Cattell et al., 1970). Generally speaking, few practical pieces of validity data are available for these factors; however, they have come out in certain second-order factor analyses of the 16 PF, and hence are mentioned here for completeness.

---

[2]Inspector Javert, from Victor Hugo's *Les Miserables,* is an excellent example of this second-order factor of compulsivity. This identification may also explain why we have chosen to emphasize the negative, rather than the positive, qualities of high scorers on it.

Clinical Examples

In this chapter we present a variety of 16 PF profiles and their interpretations. In every instance we have changed pertinent facts about the cases in order to ensure complete anonymity. Typically, the only information available to us at the time the interpretations were made was the person's age, sex, occupation, and the 16 PF profile, as well as 16 PF standardization data for each occupation tested. It is essential to have at least this much information about the person in question. Such data yields a frame of reference and offers points of comparison with which to begin a personality description. We also consider it obligatory to attempt to obtain follow-up data on cases which have been interpreted, in order to get feedback about the accuracy of the interpretations rendered. A human interpreter needs to have a data bank of clinical experience and feedback, and has to be programmed in much the same manner that a computer must, in order to produce accurate personality descriptions.

Before moving to actual examples, we shall describe the general approach used by the authors in giving a 16 PF interpretation; in all honesty, we should say that we will *attempt* to explain the process. Often it involves leaps of inference which are not clear even to us.[1]

---

[1]We are reminded here of a European chef who was famous for his recipe for making spaghetti clam sauce. When interviewed by a reporter about the secret of how he made his famous sauce, he explained: "First I clean up the kitchen getting everything in order. Next, I roll up my sleeves. Then I make clam sauce."

Steps in Interpreting a 16 PF Profile

1) We invariably look first at the indices of faking and random answering, if available, namely, the MD, Faking Bad, and Random scales. This step has become a habit, often occurring before we take cognizance of the patient's age, sex, and other identifying data. You will notice that high MD scores are frequently the first thing mentioned in our reports.

2) We then move to the second-order scores, particularly anxiety and extraversion. These provide a succinct summary of the rest of the profile. If the second-order anxiety score is elevated, you will most likely find a comment about it early in the report, for this factor is the one most indicative of psychopathology on the 16 PF. If the anxiety score is strongly depressed, we usually look at the MD score for data about the possibility that the person has faked the test.

3) Assuming that the MD and Faking Bad scores are not exceptional, we generally begin by making simple declarative assertions about the highest and lowest scores in the profile, in order of their deviation from the average. We interpret the scores as closely as possible, you'll find, being careful to specify precisely where each interpretation comes from. We try to specify every factor or combination of factors that leads to an interpretation. At this initial stage it is important for the novice to stick closely to the data.

4) As we proceed through step 3, hypotheses are formed about the nature of the problem, and usually when we have completed that step we have a good idea of the way in which the data should be integrated. Sometimes we comment on these hypotheses as we discuss the individual scale scores. But we invariably discuss them in detail after step 3 is completed. This is the stage at which the clinician's fund of clinical lore is invaluable. In the following cases you'll find comments made about certain combinations of 16 PF scores, discussion of the relationships of 16 PF scores to general personality theory, and observations on patients that we have seen in the past. Step 4 is really the quintessence of the clinician's activity, the step at which the integration of the data occurs. Hunches are formed and attempts are made at finding support for them from other 16 PF data. Many such hunches are not sustained by the data and must be discarded. In the cases

which follow we have tried to capture something of the flavor of this process of clinical integration. How successful our attempts have been, we cannot know without feedback.

5) We then attempt to summarize the case, sometimes in the form of a specific psychiatric diagnosis; however, this often proves difficult to do. People seen in practice are not as clear-cut as examples in abnormal psychology textbooks, and we frequently find ourselves not giving any diagnosis at all, but instead, summarizing the person's principal psychodynamics.

6) At this point, we attempt to compare our hypotheses about the person with other test data when available, to see if the interpretations reinforce each other. If not, adjustments must be made. Typically, in clinical practice, we work with a test battery which includes the following tests: the 16 PF, WAIS, Rorschach, MMPI, Bender-Gestalt, and, at times, almost every test in our armamentarium. It is fun to do blind analyses based on the 16 PF alone, but in the end *all* data on the patient must be integrated.

7) Finally, in every case we make a concerted effort to obtain follow-up data on the person. We feel strongly that feedback is necessary if one is to become an expert interpreter. If we diagnose someone as an aggressive sociopath, we consider it essential to know whether the referring psychiatrist concurs with us, whether the official hospital diagnosis is in agreement, and whether the case history supports our diagnosis. In the cases that follow you'll notice that there are a few patients on whom follow-up data is only minimal. We have a hunch that you'll find these cases as frustrating as we do— fascinating people about whom we don't know the eventual outcome. A dedicated clinician will attempt to obtain extensive follow-up data whenever possible in order to check his accuracy and improve his predictions.

The bulk of our experience has been with normals, neurotics, and character disorders, the very people with whom the 16 PF was designed to produce good results. Our experience with psychotic patients is more limited because of the clinical settings in which we have worked. It may well be that the Clinical Analysis Questionnaire (Delhees & Cattell, 1970) will prove more valuable with severely disturbed people; it is still a relatively new instrument. But we remain confident of the 16 PF's usefulness with normal and neurotic cases as well as with personality disorders, the samples from which the bulk of the following cases were drawn.

Each case will be prefaced by its 16 PF profile, a brief rationale for its inclusion, and the presenting problem. The interpretations which follow are, in all honesty, not a good sample of interpretations used in clinical work. They are far more verbose and detailed than that purpose ordinarily requires. In writing profile interpretations for this book, we actually took short clinical reports and expanded them for didactic purposes. Our aim was that of explaining and making explicit each step in the inferences that we drew. If we had the slightest doubt about the reader's understanding the source of an interpretation, we spelled it out in greater detail. Because of this meticulousness, you may find that the reports are more repetitious at times than you'd like. Perhaps this is a result of many years of teaching. You soon find in such a setting that you must usually say things two or three times before you feel you've been understood.

We have taken great care to be consistent in the labels given to factors, especially in the earlier examples. In cases after number 10, we permit ourselves more liberty in using names for the factors that are somewhat more appropriate to the nuance of the case.

You will also find that we frequently don't follow the steps that we've outlined for ourselves at the beginning of the chapter. For example, most of the cases presented are at least five years old, and this means that we don't have Random and Faking Bad scores for them. Also, we very frequently infer the level of the second-order scores, not from the calculated value, but from the pattern of the primaries. This is especially the case with anxiety. After a time you get a feel for the second-order factors which somehow transcends the calculated value. Consequently, we often talk about the second-order scores mainly in terms of the primaries.

Case I: Mr. Barry Q.

A Man with Psychosomatic Symptoms

PRESENTING PROBLEM:

Mr. Barry Q's 16 PF profile was given to the writers as a completely blind profile. The following interpretation was made in the absence of any information about the man, except for his occupation (radioman in the merchant marine, a job held also by his father), and his age of 29.

IN-DEPTH INTERPRETATION:

This man is bright (B $=$ 8) and has good ability to bind anxiety ($Q_3 =$ 9). There is tough, masculine realism in his personality makeup, a lack of emotional sensitivity (I $=$ 2), and a concrete, practical approach to tasks rather than a tendency to daydream (M $=$ 1).

As you'd expect of someone in his position, he shows low anxiety on all factors entering into the measurement of anxiety: He has a 7 on C (ego strength), a 4 on L (suspiciousness), little guilt proneness (O $=$ 3), high obsessive-compulsivity ($Q_3 =$ 9), and, finally, little evidence of free-floating anxiety ($Q_4 =$ 1). The MD score (7) shows that he may have tried to present a favorable picture of himself, but not to such a degree as to make the 16 PF protocol invalid.

Anger is a problem. E— (submissiveness), coupled with Q_1+ (rebelliousness) and N+ (shrewdness), suggests that he expresses hostility in covert, intellectualized ways, rather than through confrontation. The high Q_1 also suggests difficulty with authority figures.

We might wonder about the adequacy of superego introjection, given the G of 6 (group conformity), an O of only 3 (guilt proneness), an F of 5 (impulsivity), and a Q_3 of 9 (ability to bind anxiety). The general picture, though, is not that of a person with poor superego controls, even though superego introjection (O $=$ 3) is low, since Q_3 is elevated and F and G are average. It is of particular interest that this man's father is also a radioman. This paternal identification or introjected ego ideal is reflected in the low I (2), the above average H (7), as well as the low M (1). I (tough-mindedness), H (boldness), and M (imagination) are the three factors which we believe deal primarily with masculine strivings on the 16 PF.

Some acting-out behavior would also not be unexpected with the high H and average F.

Barry Q. appears to be a very sophisticated, manipulative person with a good deal of experience in social relations (N = 8, B = 8, G = 6, O = 3). High Q_2 (self-sufficiency) also points to good work habits, especially since in this case it is accompanied by high intelligence and disciplined character traits.

In short, at this point in time he appears to have few problems with anxiety, depression, or impulse control. But we wonder about his need to deny any feelings of anxiety to the extent that he does (Q_4 = 1). We feel that the major area of his vulnerability lies in the direction of psychosomatic symptoms. This is inferred because of his very low scores on I (emotional sensitivity) and M (imagination). As we noted briefly in Chapter 4, clinical experience suggests that men with unusually low scores on I and M as well as those with high scores seem to be vulnerable to developing ulcers and similar symptoms under stress. Low M implies a highly practical approach to life, so that M— people ordinarily cannot resort to fantasy as a defense against stressful situations. Here, the low I connotes tough masculinity and a denial of feelings. Such a Spartan attitude frequently serves as a defense against anxiety. We all know "hard-boiled" executives who are actually very anxious and sensitive. Under continuing stress their defense breaks down, and such men may develop psychosomatic symptoms. These symptoms may also serve as an outlet for secondary gains; symptoms often get one out of unpleasant situations without the necessity of examining one's value systems.

The possibility of acting-out behavior cannot be ruled out in this case, since his basic personality structure is not highly introverted and his ego ideal clearly emphasizes tough masculinity.

Because of the paucity of data on this man a diagnosis was not attempted; however, psychosis or anxiety neurosis can probably be ruled out.

FOLLOW-UP:

We were amazed to find that Barry Q. had been missing work two out of five mornings for several months

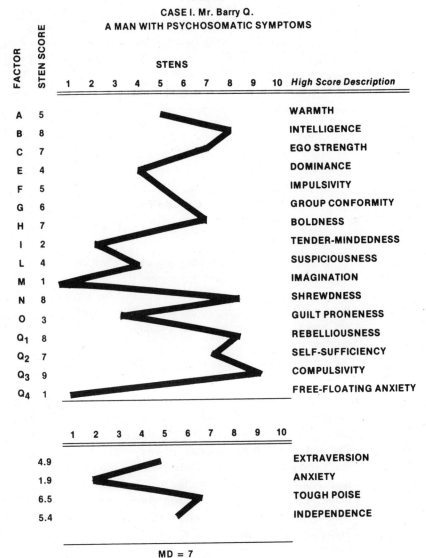

FIGURE 6-1

CASE I. Mr. Barry Q.

A MAN WITH PSYCHOSOMATIC SYMPTOMS

FACTOR	STEN SCORE		High Score Description
A	5		WARMTH
B	8		INTELLIGENCE
C	7		EGO STRENGTH
E	4		DOMINANCE
F	5		IMPULSIVITY
G	6		GROUP CONFORMITY
H	7		BOLDNESS
I	2		TENDER-MINDEDNESS
L	4		SUSPICIOUSNESS
M	1		IMAGINATION
N	8		SHREWDNESS
O	3		GUILT PRONENESS
Q_1	8		REBELLIOUSNESS
Q_2	7		SELF-SUFFICIENCY
Q_3	9		COMPULSIVITY
Q_4	1		FREE-FLOATING ANXIETY

STENS 1 2 3 4 5 6 7 8 9 10

4.9		EXTRAVERSION
1.9		ANXIETY
6.5		TOUGH POISE
5.4		INDEPENDENCE

1 2 3 4 5 6 7 8 9 10

MD = 7

101

because of what he called "real bad headaches." A confounding problem lay in the fact that he was eligible to receive a substantial pension if he did not return to duty because of medical reasons. Unfortunately, absenteeism cannot be tolerated in his position. He was medically retired, and is receiving a disability pension.

As with the case in the first part of the book, we can't claim that you'll have this sort of luck in every case in which you use the 16 PF. But it does show the utility of the test.

Case II: Captain Tommy T.

A Case of Reactive Depression, Not Picked Up by the 16 PF

The following is a case in which we were not able to successfully detect the person's problem from a 16 PF, even with much knowledge of the case. We include it partly because it's interesting, and also because we like to admit occasionally that we don't bat a thousand in our clinical descriptions.

PRESENTING PROBLEM:

Captain Tommy T. was a check pilot for a major airline. After he had failed a pilot whom he was checking out, he and the pilot got into a dispute about the decision. The pilot being checked said, "If you're so darned good, why don't you show me how?" The Captain agreed to this, with the idea of demonstrating how the landing approach should be made. Captain Tommy T. then proceeded to foul up the landing approach himself, and received an official reprimand. This blow to his perfectionistic standards depressed him so much that he required hospitalization and was subsequently removed from flight duties. A few months afterwards the first 16 PF was given, and the interpretation was made blindly. About a year later, when the Captain was being considered for reinstatement, a second 16 PF was given, and that interpretation is included for comparison purposes. This second interpretation, however, was made with considerable knowledge of the case.

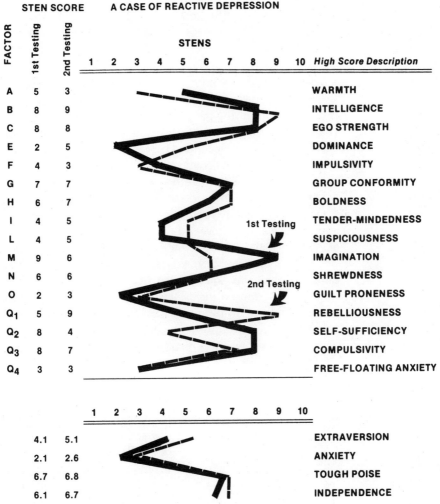

FIGURE 6-2

CASE II. CAPTAIN TOMMY T.

A CASE OF REACTIVE DEPRESSION

STEN SCORE

FACTOR	1st Testing	2nd Testing	High Score Description
A	5	3	WARMTH
B	8	9	INTELLIGENCE
C	8	8	EGO STRENGTH
E	2	5	DOMINANCE
F	4	3	IMPULSIVITY
G	7	7	GROUP CONFORMITY
H	6	7	BOLDNESS
I	4	5	TENDER-MINDEDNESS
L	4	5	SUSPICIOUSNESS
M	9	6	IMAGINATION
N	6	6	SHREWDNESS
O	2	3	GUILT PRONENESS
Q_1	5	9	REBELLIOUSNESS
Q_2	8	4	SELF-SUFFICIENCY
Q_3	8	7	COMPULSIVITY
Q_4	3	3	FREE-FLOATING ANXIETY

	4.1	5.1	EXTRAVERSION
	2.1	2.6	ANXIETY
	6.7	6.8	TOUGH POISE
	6.1	6.7	INDEPENDENCE

MD (1st Testing) = 6

MD (2nd Testing) = 12

103

FIRST IN-DEPTH INTERPRETATION:

A review of this 16 PF indicates that, as with most pilots, he is highly intelligent (B = 8), tough and masculine (I = 4), and emotionally stable (C = 8). Too, he shows good ability to bind anxiety and much compulsivity (Q3 = 8). The Q2 of 8 implies that he has high self-sufficiency; this almost invariably accompanies good work habits. It is unusual for a pilot to make an E as low as 2; they usually have little trouble in confronting people or in expressing angry impulses. His hostility is not primarily directed toward authority figures, or intellectualized, since the Q1 (rebelliousness) is only 5. He is a relatively high group conformist (G = 7). An O of 2 suggests weakness in superego introjection, although control factors in this area are present: that is, F (impulsivity) is only 4, Q3 (ability to bind anxiety) is 8, and G is 7. All of these have important bearings on various aspects of superego control and in the introjection of perfectionistic standards.

The M (9) is highly unusual for a pilot. It indicates impracticality and dissociative tendencies which could seriously interfere with his job performance. His MD (6) is somewhat above average, but not enough to invalidate the 16 PF profile. The second-order anxiety score of 2.1 is so low as to raise the possibility of a massive denial of anxiety, but the MD score contraindicates such a conclusion.

His profile, in contrast with Mr. Barry Q. in Case I, leads us to believe that he is not particularly vulnerable to psychosomatic symptoms. He gives the impression of being a submissive and accommodating person (E = 2), and could perhaps be admitting to feelings of depression (F = 4). The central psychodynamics seem to revolve around an inability to express id impulses, especially anger, in a person with a perfectionistic and rigid ego-ideal (Q3 = 8).

In short, the relatively high G, low F, and high Q3 suggest an obsessive-compulsive personality who is vulnerable to depression. There would not appear to be any particular diagnosis in this case; the record is not psychotic, and is far from being the typical neurotic profile, since none of the anxiety indicators is elevated. We could speculate that the main problem is depression, but it isn't all that clear.

SECOND IN-DEPTH INTERPRETATION:

This interpretation was made to contrast the first and second 16 PF profiles. The attending psychiatrist felt that depression was no longer a serious problem, and wondered if there was concurrence that Captain Tommy T. could return to work.

This time the Motivational Distortion score was 12; therefore, we must question the validity of the test scores, particularly the anxiety indicators. It was evident that he was attempting to fake good in order to be returned to duty. Again, his intelligence is high, and he demonstrates good superego control; not only is he above average on group conformity (G = 7), but he also shows much impulse control (F = 3) and above average ability to bind anxiety (Q3 = 7). He also evidences few signs of guilt proneness or chronic worrying (O = 3). In the second testing, he shows significantly more evidence of hostility toward authority figures (Q1 = 9) and less submissiveness (E = 5). This is puzzling, but perhaps in the treatment he was receiving, the psychiatrist had encouraged him to ventilate his anger by expressing anti-establishment sentiments. He is also less dissociative than before since his M has gone from 9 to 6, and he is more group dependent since Q2 has changed from 8 to 4. In general, though, the profiles are basically similar in configuration, since 11 of the 16 factors have not changed by more than one point.

FOLLOW-UP:

The psychiatric evaluation stated that the diagnosis considered at the time of the first evaluation was that of severe, mixed psychoneurosis, with anxiety and depression. It was noted during the administration of the first 16 PF that the Captain sighed a great deal, sat quietly with little movement for half an hour, and seemed very depressed.

However, we must admit that we didn't really pick up the depression or anxiety from the 16 PF. The statement in the first interpretation about the possibility of depression was largely a lucky guess which was thrown in for consideration. Of course, in retrospect, all the elements are there for such a diagnosis in the 16 PF record, but it proved difficult to synthesize them into the precise diagnosis needed.

The last information that we have showed that Captain Tommy T. had not yet been returned to flying duties.

Case III: Mr. Charles M.

A Schizoid Personality

PRESENTING PROBLEM:

This 34-year-old sailor was referred for a personality evaluation. His behavior on shipboard was decidedly odd and began getting him into more and more difficulty. He wandered around deck at odd hours with a peculiar look in his eyes. The 16 PF was administered at intake; the following personality description was based only on the profile, and not on materials collected later. Those will be discussed after the 16 PF interpretation.

IN-DEPTH INTERPRETATION:

The low MD score shows that he approached the test honestly. There is only one score as high as 8, and no 9's or 10's. The highest score is on self-sufficiency (Q_2). Except for A (warmth), where he is average, he is significantly on the introverted side on all the major personality factors which load the second-order extraversion factor, namely, an F (impulsivity) and H (boldness) of 2, as well as a 2 on extraversion itself. These scores suggest a good deal of shyness and a serious approach to life. Along with this is much emotional sensitivity ($I = 7$). His low N implies limited social experience and naivete. Moreover, he is not a dominant, aggressive person ($E = 3$), but instead appears to be especially submissive and accommodating. The low E, coupled with an H of only 2, suggests much difficulty in the area of assertiveness.

The highest anxiety score appears on guilt proneness ($O = 7$). His ego strength score is somewhat below average ($C = 4$), as is his ability to bind anxiety ($Q_3 = 4$). There is no evidence of marked free-floating anxiety ($Q_4 = 4$). With regard to superego control, he scored a 7 on G (group conformity) and a 2 on F; this suggests great responsibility. Q_3 is somewhat below average, and O is 7, which implies a harsh, rigidly introjected superego.

There is little evidence of an aggressive character disorder in this profile. In such disorders we expect an extraverted personality with an emphasis on hostility ($E+$, $L+$, Q_1+) and impulsivity and bravado ($F+$, $H+$). All these would describe an energetic, immature, risk-taking and

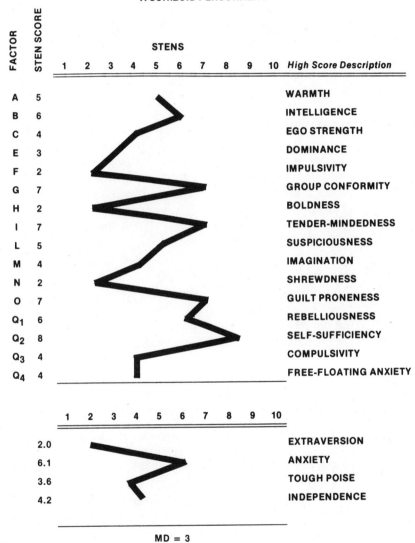

FIGURE 6-3
CASE III. MR. CHARLES M.
A SCHIZOID PERSONALITY

MD = 3

impulsive person, prone to act out his conflicts. Such a syndrome would ordinarily be coupled with difficulties in superego control (G—, O—, F+, Q3—).

Neither is the 16 PF profile characteristic of neurotic patients; they usually have elevated anxiety scores, and that is not the case here. Instead, the emphasis is on superego concerns, guilt, worrying, identity problems, sensitivity, submissiveness, and shyness. The profile suggests a psychiatric disorder of a schizoid type.

FOLLOW-UP:

The interview and testing administered to Mr. Charles M. after the 16 PF show a striking degree of psychopathology. In interview his speech was coherent, but odd and rapid. If uninterrupted he would continue talking almost incessantly. The content of his verbalizations showed over-concern with religion and morals. His writings also reflected this preoccupation.

The Rorschach was most unusual. There was no human movement, and no reference to people of any kind. But there was a striking preoccupation with human anatomy. Several times he confused male sexual organs that he saw on the Rorschach with female ones, and vice versa. Throughout the Rorschach he prefaced his responses with "I don't know." This remark reflected his lack of confidence in himself.

The patient volunteered to write an autobiography, without any urging from the examiner. This was an amazing document. A few excerpts are of interest:

I remember when I first started school that when they all got up to sing My Country Tis of Thee that I cried out loud. I can't sing and the whole class laughed and laughed until I started crying. I felt out of place in a strange place and I didn't know what to do.

Another excerpt:

I am now only learning the hard grim facts of life today and I am still yet very much in the dark on many things pertaining to a woman. When I lost my power my faith went from God, and I have lived some terrible times in my life since the time I have been without power and without a girl . . . .

In reference to my rapid or gradual sexual destruction as I call it first had taken place on January 16, 1955, but as of the exact day I do not recall . . . .

He was not found suitable for further military duty, and was duly discharged from the Navy on medical and psychiatric grounds.

Case IV: Mr. Albert P.

A Manic in Remission

The following case, inherently interesting though it is, shows the importance of scoring the MD scale. Motivational Distortion in this instance obscures the dynamics of the case.

PRESENTING PROBLEM:

Mr. Albert P. was 37, and had been an air traffic controller in a large government agency. His position involved a good deal of responsibility and stress. Three years ago he suffered a psychotic episode, and was subsequently diagnosed as manic-depressive psychosis, manic type, based on thorough psychiatric and psychological evaluations. The course of his illness was fairly brief, and after a series of electroconvulsive treatments he was discharged as being in remission. When he applied for another position, a current psychological evaluation was obtained as a means of determining the degree to which he had overcome his illness.

IN-DEPTH INTERPRETATION:

A review of the profile indicates a Motivational Distortion score of 12. This is unusually high and clearly shows that he is trying to present himself in a favorable light. As we would expect, accompanying this high MD is a denial of almost all anxiety symptoms—for example, he makes a C of 9 (ego strength), an L of 2 (suspiciousness), an O of 4 (guilt proneness), a Q_3 of 8 (ability to bind anxiety), and a Q_4 of 2 (free-floating anxiety). All of these scores are near the ends yielding the lowest anxiety. Given the high MD and the low anxiety scores which usually accompany high Motivational

FIGURE 6-4
CASE IV. MR. ALBERT P.
A MANIC IN REMISSION

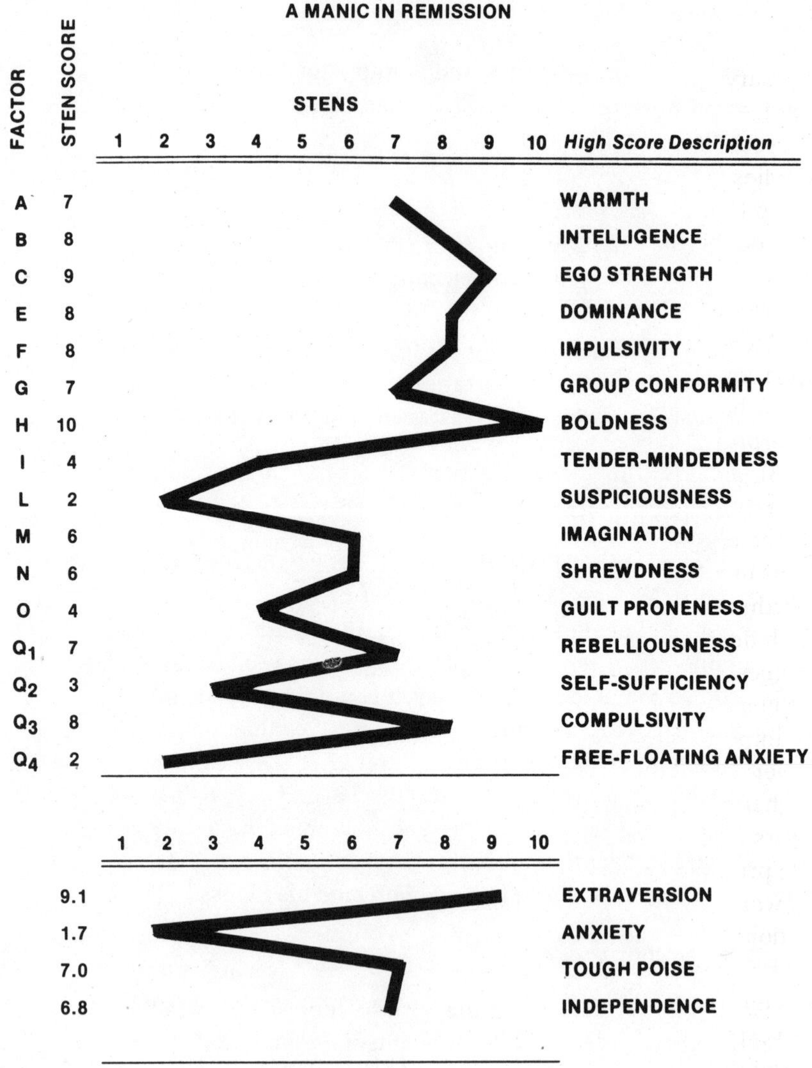

FACTOR	STEN SCORE	STENS 1 2 3 4 5 6 7 8 9 10	High Score Description
A	7		WARMTH
B	8		INTELLIGENCE
C	9		EGO STRENGTH
E	8		DOMINANCE
F	8		IMPULSIVITY
G	7		GROUP CONFORMITY
H	10		BOLDNESS
I	4		TENDER-MINDEDNESS
L	2		SUSPICIOUSNESS
M	6		IMAGINATION
N	6		SHREWDNESS
O	4		GUILT PRONENESS
Q_1	7		REBELLIOUSNESS
Q_2	3		SELF-SUFFICIENCY
Q_3	8		COMPULSIVITY
Q_4	2		FREE-FLOATING ANXIETY

	1 2 3 4 5 6 7 8 9 10	
9.1		EXTRAVERSION
1.7		ANXIETY
7.0		TOUGH POISE
6.8		INDEPENDENCE

MD = 12

110

Distortion, it is hard to say anything about the level of anxiety he is actually feeling in this case.

We then turn to the other factors. As indicated by the second-order extraversion score of 9.1, all of his primary scores on it are in the expected direction: $A = 7$, $F = 8$, $H = 10$, and $Q_2 = 3$. Apparently he considers it advantageous to answer in a highly extraverted direction. The B of 8 implies fairly high intelligence. An E of 8 coupled with a Q_1 of 7 and H of 10 suggests that he is aggressive and assertive, and acts out his angry impulses under stress.

Except for the presence of the high MD score, we would be forced to conclude that he shows no particular problems with anxiety. But we cannot be so certain with this high an MD. Character problems appear to be in evidence, since he admits to having problems with angry feelings, as interpreted above, and he is highly impulsive and immature ($F = 8$), as well as a high risk taker ($H = 10$) and tough-minded ($I = 4$). This combination of scores suggests that he has introjected a highly masculine ego ideal, which is being presented to us in his 16 PF profile. The Q_2 (self-sufficiency) of 3 is noteworthy: the position that he is hoping to reoccupy calls for a high degree of self-sufficiency, but his Q_2 score on the 16 PF suggests much group dependency and a need for help and support from others. Finally, on the critical factor of cortertia, so important to effective work in air traffic control, he gets a lower score than others in that profession, although he's higher than people in the general population. Compared to his peers he is ruled by his feelings rather than his intellect. On the primaries entering into this score, he earns scores of 7 on A (warmth), a 4 on I (tough masculinity), and an M of 6 (imagination).

What we see on the profile, then, is an attempt to present a highly favorable picture of himself. Nevertheless, certain character traits do come through. His major dynamics seem to center about his highly masculine ego ideal, difficulty in handling angry impulses, and a strong tendency to externalize his conflicts.

It would be difficult to make a diagnosis in this case, since the MD is so high and the anxiety scores so low. Ordinarily, we would suggest that he should be seen for a full psychological evaluation. This is one case where a single testing, under such defensiveness, is simply not sufficient.

He's not a neurotic; the typical neurotic profile is not so heavily distorted and has much evidence of anxiety. Psychosis also does not seem likely.

FOLLOW-UP:

This man was not returned to his original position, although he was given another less critical and responsible position with the same agency. It appears that his psychosis remains in remission.

It is interesting that an MMPI which was available on this man was similarly within normal limits, even with respect to the validity scales. Consequently, we conclude that the 16 PF at least was successful in detecting his attempt to fake good. His MMPI Hypomania score is very nearly beyond "normal" limits, and this is what one might expect from someone with a manic disorder in his history.

Case V: Richard M.

A Paranoid Personality?

PRESENTING PROBLEM:

Mr. Richard M. was a final quality control inspector for a large corporation. He was referred for psychological evaluation because of increasing difficulty in keeping his temper. He had never attacked anyone, but once, in disgust, he had smashed a tray of dishes in the company cafeteria. This erratic behavior led to a request on the part of the company physician for an evaluation, since he was in a position of considerable responsibility.

IN-DEPTH INTERPRETATION:

This man's profile indicates that he has very low emotional stability ($C = 1$). Guilt proneness is also remarkably high ($O = 10$), indicating that he is a chronic worrier. Free-floating anxiety is also at maximum ($Q_4 = 10$). The Q_3 of 1 suggests that he has little ability to use obsessive-compulsive mechanisms to bind anxiety. Finally, on the last of the anxiety primaries, L, he earns a score of 8, showing a strong tendency to project and displace heavily. We often

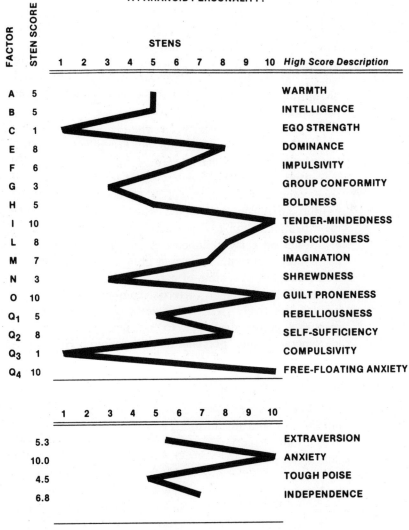

FIGURE 6-5
CASE V. RICHARD M.
A PARANOID PERSONALITY?

FACTOR	STEN SCORE	STENS	High Score Description
		1 2 3 4 5 6 7 8 9 10	
A	5		WARMTH
B	5		INTELLIGENCE
C	1		EGO STRENGTH
E	8		DOMINANCE
F	6		IMPULSIVITY
G	3		GROUP CONFORMITY
H	5		BOLDNESS
I	10		TENDER-MINDEDNESS
L	8		SUSPICIOUSNESS
M	7		IMAGINATION
N	3		SHREWDNESS
O	10		GUILT PRONENESS
Q_1	5		REBELLIOUSNESS
Q_2	8		SELF-SUFFICIENCY
Q_3	1		COMPULSIVITY
Q_4	10		FREE-FLOATING ANXIETY

	1 2 3 4 5 6 7 8 9 10	
5.3		EXTRAVERSION
10.0		ANXIETY
4.5		TOUGH POISE
6.8		INDEPENDENCE

MD = 3

113

prefer to call L+ "anxious insecurity" rather than "suspiciousness," since it is a primary component of the second-order anxiety factor. L+ seems to measure anxiety as much as pure tendencies toward projection, hence the term "anxious insecurity." As you'd expect, since almost all of the anxiety indicators are up, the second-order anxiety factor itself is at the highest possible score. This degree of discomfort makes us wonder about how much his personal problems and the disrupting effects of anxiety are interfering with his ability to perform effectively.

He is very markedly emotionally sensitive (I), especially considering the job he occupies. We can also hypothesize that this maximum score on I, combined with the maximum second-order anxiety score and high scores on the anger factors (E and L), imply a good deal of sensitivity to hostility in this man, coupled with a strong mother-figure identification. High I scores are believed to spring from an overprotected early childhood in which there has not been much interaction with one's peer group, or much participation in the rough and tumble of everyday life. Further, the comparatively low score on cortertia, combined with a Q3 of 1, implies relatively few effective cognitive controls. His response patterns appear to be largely determined by idiosyncractic and personal considerations. High cortertia implies a person capable of making rapid, accurate cognitive decisions when necessary. It is essential in occupations where fast responses to a changing situation are necessary. In such jobs one must be alert, ready to respond, open to new information, and able to adjust quickly under pressure of time. Persons low on cortertia are often not able to do this on a sustained basis.

The combination of 8's on E and L suggests problems in handling anger. A mixture of overwhelming anxiety, low ego strength and high emotional sensitivity as well as difficulty with anger suggests paranoid ideation in this man. A punitive superego is implied by the low group conformity (G = 3), accompanied by the maximum score on guilt proneness (O = 10).

In many ways he looks like a severe anxiety neurotic; however, his major difficulty with angry impulses (E+, L+) makes it apparent that he does not quite fit this picture. These dynamics would be better fit by a paranoid personality, since some of the basic dynamics frequently encountered are psychosexual problems, many angry impulses, low ego strength, and displacement and projection—all found in this case.

FOLLOW-UP:

Beyond the fact that this man was not retained in his job, we know little about what actually happened to him. However, we do have access to psychiatric and psychological reports, done independently of the present evaluation.

The psychiatric evaluation pictures an emotion-starved life as a child; the patient grew up in an orphanage. The psychiatrist notes feelings that people were against him, that they were mocking him, and a certain degree of thought disturbance. The diagnosis made was that of paranoid schizophrenia. The psychological report mentions excessive vigilance, generalized suspiciousness, and mistrust of others. The diagnosis made by the psychologist was that of an ambulatory paranoid schizophrenic. Upon further evaluation a year later, he was diagnosed a paranoid personality.

Case VI: Mr. Donald K.

A Case of Claustrophobia

PRESENTING PROBLEM:

Mr. Donald K., a 32-year-old married man with two children, was the chief security officer for a large building. His actual work consisted of observing a number of TV monitors to check for possible fires and burglaries. He also had to continually monitor the elevator controls for proper operation. Since the building was enormous and crowded, his job involved much responsibility. In 1972 he began to feel that he was approaching a "nervous breakdown." The symptoms were those of free-floating anxiety and phobias, particularly claustrophobia. This was particularly troublesome to him in his work, for he worked in an inner room in the building which served as the control center for the whole building operation. He admitted to an examining psychiatrist that he had been claustrophobic to a degree throughout his life. Nevertheless, he has had little or no difficulty on his job previously; however, with the intensification of the phobic symptoms, he found it

FIGURE 6-6
CASE VI. MR. DONALD K.
A CASE OF CLAUSTROPHOBIA

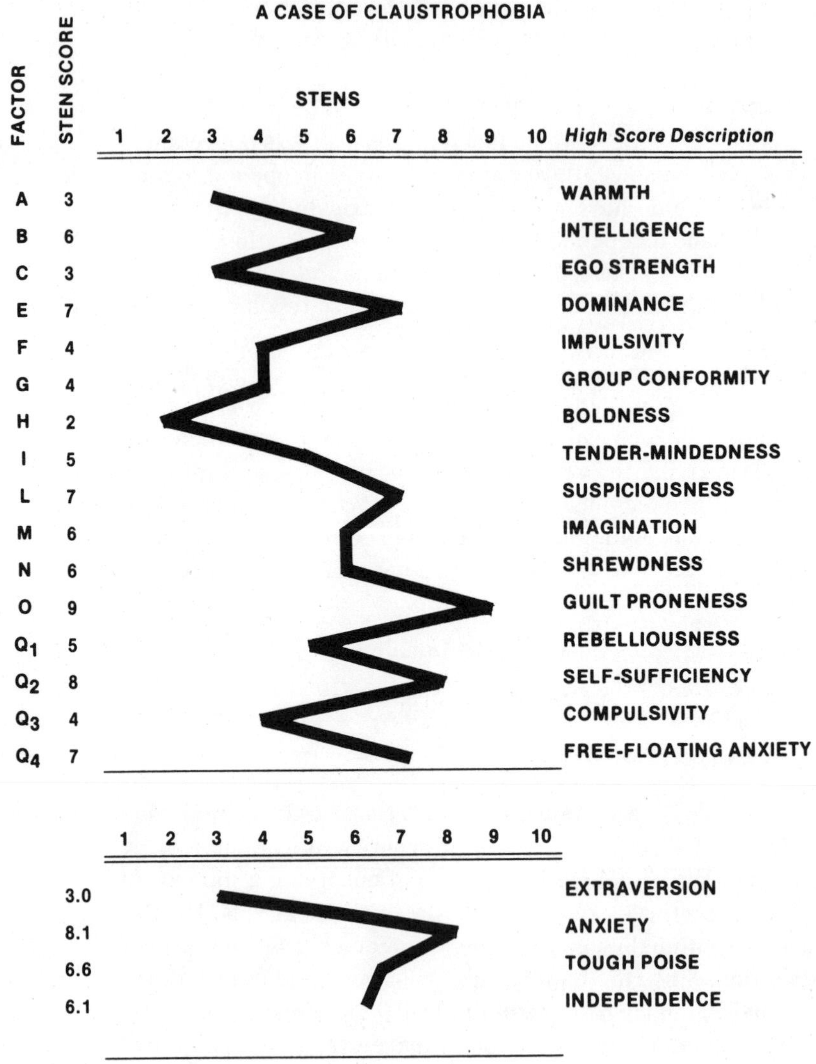

FACTOR	STEN SCORE	High Score Description
A	3	WARMTH
B	6	INTELLIGENCE
C	3	EGO STRENGTH
E	7	DOMINANCE
F	4	IMPULSIVITY
G	4	GROUP CONFORMITY
H	2	BOLDNESS
I	5	TENDER-MINDEDNESS
L	7	SUSPICIOUSNESS
M	6	IMAGINATION
N	6	SHREWDNESS
O	9	GUILT PRONENESS
Q_1	5	REBELLIOUSNESS
Q_2	8	SELF-SUFFICIENCY
Q_3	4	COMPULSIVITY
Q_4	7	FREE-FLOATING ANXIETY

	High Score Description
3.0	EXTRAVERSION
8.1	ANXIETY
6.6	TOUGH POISE
6.1	INDEPENDENCE

MD = 4

difficult to perform his duties. The psychiatric evaluation was requested to determine the patient's fitness for the job, and the 16 PF was administered pursuant to that determination.

IN-DEPTH INTERPRETATION:

The outstanding problems seem to occur with respect to the second-order factor of anxiety, on which his score was 8.1. On O (guilt proneness and chronic worrying), his score was 9, and on Q4 (free-floating anxiety), he made a 7. We know that high anxiety scores are rare in people in his occupation. Moreover, an L (suspiciousness or anxious insecurity) of 7 combined with a very high O indicates that he tends to project a good deal. Evidence of uncontained anxiety is further reinforced by the Q3 (ability to bind anxiety) of 4. On the remaining anxiety score, C or ego strength, he has a score of only 3; this reflects instability and low ego strength.

His score on A (warmth) of 3 indicates that he is not a warm person. For someone in his job, his M (the Walter Mitty factor) of 6 is above average, suggesting that he tends to cope with his apprehensions by dissociation. The lack of warmth also points to introversion, shown by his 3 on the second-order extraversion factor. His pattern of scores on the primaries that make it up, namely, an A of 3, an F of 4, an H of 2, and a Q2 of 8, also reflect his introverted nature.

Particularly relevant is his very low score on H, which indicates shyness, or, as we call it, "dispositional timidity." We prefer the latter term since there appears to be a substantial hereditary component in this factor. H— indicates high threat reactivity; and coupled with the O of 9 and the strong feelings of anxiety from almost every possible source, it strongly emphasizes the great apprehensions and susceptibility to anxiety found in this man. He is terribly vulnerable to environmental stresses and unable to obtain gratification from others because of his shyness.

The combination of E+ and L+ is troublesome. E measures aggressiveness for the most part, but when coupled with high L we frequently conclude that id impulses are improperly handled. Anger is a problem for him and so he resorts to displacement and projection. In the study of psychopathology, it is frequently observed that difficulty with hostility is a major dynamic around which paranoid defenses are established. Since Donald K. is insecure (L+) and timid (H—), and has established poor trust relationships, it is not surprising that he has become introverted, and feels guilty about his angry feelings. We see here the common neurotic pattern of G— (low group conformity) and O+ (guilt proneness), where the person behaves in unconventional ways, and is subsequently punished by the archaic superego for these liberties.

With regard to diagnosis, it is unlikely that he is psychotic. Typically, chronic schizophrenic profiles on the 16 PF indicate anxiety coming from only one or two sources, not from all of them, as is the case here. His great anxiety suggests that he is still trying to cope and that he is suffering from an anxiety neurosis, or something similar. With regard to prognosis, it is clear that he needs psychotherapy. His high anxiety would motivate him to seek professional help. Unfortunately, it has been our experience that anxiety of this magnitude in an H— person is difficult to change permanently, but perhaps he could be helped to manage his anxiety better.

We have serious reservations about whether he can return to his job and function effectively. His anxiety is simply too high and his ego defenses too ineffective.

FOLLOW-UP:

It is noteworthy that he didn't return to the job, simply, as he said, because he "couldn't stand being cooped up in that little room" again.

Case VII: Mr. Kenneth L.

A Personality Disorder

PRESENTING PROBLEM:

Mr. Kenneth L. was a slight, 25-year-old man applying for the job of sonar operator in the Merchant Marine. This is a highly touchy occupation, and a question arose as to his psychological suitability for the job, even though he appeared to have the educational qualifications necessary. The referral question was whether the man had sufficient stability to carry out this responsible job.

IN-DEPTH INTERPRETATION:

An inspection of the 16 PF reveals that he has high free-floating anxiety ($Q_4 = 9$) coupled with marked impulsivity and immaturity, as indicated by an F of 10. Apart from the high Q_4, the other anxiety indicators are not unusual: C (ego strength) is 5, L (suspiciousness or anxious insecurity) is 6, O (guilt proneness) is also 6. Q_3 (compulsivity) is particularly important in his occupation, and his score of 4 on that scale is problematically low. The MD score of 7 is above average, which suggests that the amount of anxiety that he admits to in this profile is a minimal estimate of the actual anxiety that he's feeling.

He is a highly dominant and aggressive person ($E = 8$) as well as a high risk-taker ($H = 9$). Further, he is highly extraverted, as evidenced by his second-order extraversion score of 10; his scores on extraversion are all in the positive direction for that factor (A+, F+, H+, and Q_2—). Particularly troublesome is his high score on group dependency ($Q_2 = 2$). Someone who requires a lot of interaction with others to gratify his dependency needs often does not work out well in an occupation requiring high self-sufficiency and the ability to work alone. In addition, low Q_2 generally implies poor work habits. We must also be concerned about his marked impulsivity ($F = 10$) and the aggressiveness ($E = 8$) that he shows. These hint that he might well tend to act out his conflicts in crucial situations when under stress, clearly not a good characteristic in someone applying for the job he's seeking.

There are many problems apparent in his 16 PF profile which make it difficult to pinpoint a diagnosis in this case. This man has only one unusually high anxiety score, on Q_4, and none of the other anxiety indicators is remarkable. The high H of 9 indicates that he is very adventurous and shows much lower threat reactivity than do most neurotics.

We conclude, therefore, that the case is either a neurosis or a character disorder or a neurosis with character defects. The choice would seem to be the last, since Q_4 is elevated. However, we couldn't rule out the possibility of a character disorder, since the outstanding peaks on the profile are F+ (impulsivity) and H+ (boldness). These generally indicate character problems in an extraverted, hysterical

FIGURE 6-7

CASE VII. MR. KENNETH L.

A PERSONALITY DISORDER

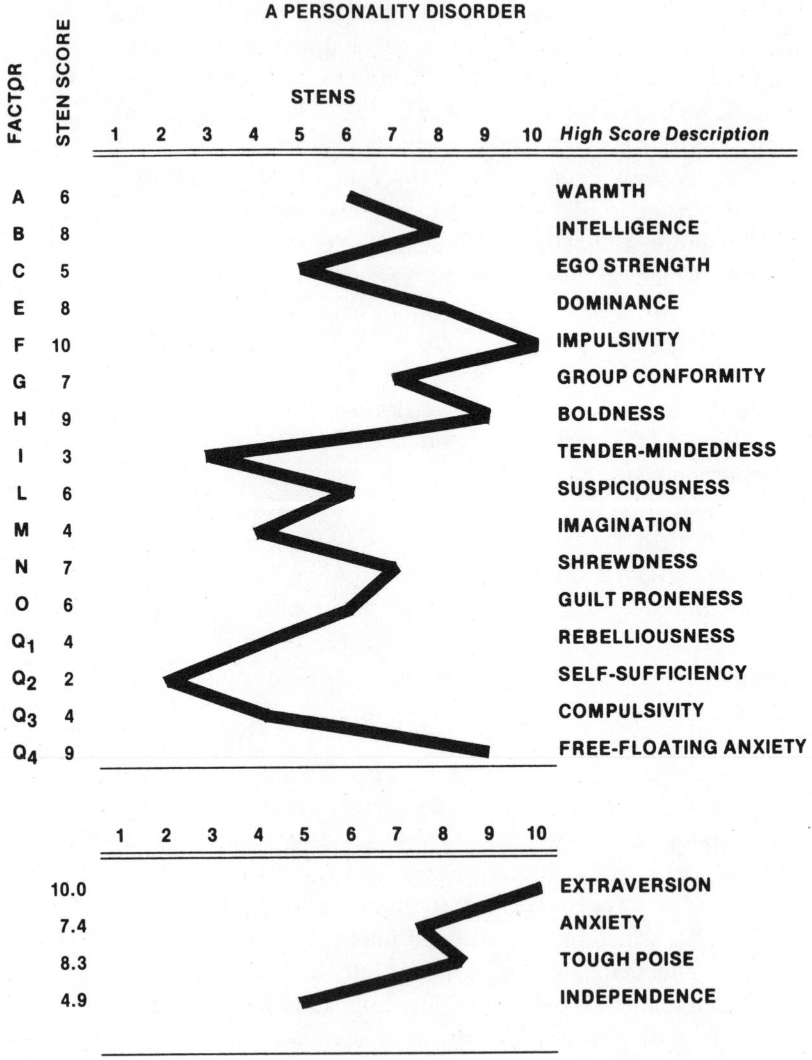
FACTOR
STEN SCORE
STENS
1 2 3 4 5 6 7 8 9 10
High Score Description
A 6 WARMTH
B 8 INTELLIGENCE
C 5 EGO STRENGTH
E 8 DOMINANCE
F 10 IMPULSIVITY
G 7 GROUP CONFORMITY
H 9 BOLDNESS
I 3 TENDER-MINDEDNESS
L 6 SUSPICIOUSNESS
M 4 IMAGINATION
N 7 SHREWDNESS
O 6 GUILT PRONENESS
Q1 4 REBELLIOUSNESS
Q2 2 SELF-SUFFICIENCY
Q3 4 COMPULSIVITY
Q4 9 FREE-FLOATING ANXIETY
1 2 3 4 5 6 7 8 9 10
10.0 EXTRAVERSION
7.4 ANXIETY
8.3 TOUGH POISE
4.9 INDEPENDENCE

MD = 7

personality structure. We do not think that he is a sociopath, though, since his G of 7 indicates relatively high group conformity, coupled with high average superego introjection ($O = 6$). He also evidences a highly athletic ego ideal ($H = 9$, $I = 3$, $M = 4$), unlike that of most neurotics.

We'd guess that he might have a chance at improvement, provided that he could be gotten into psychotherapy. Our experience with many patients over the years is that men who are low I and M as well as high H tend to avoid seeking professional help for their problems, since they consider such attempts as unmanly and as revealing weakness in themselves which is alien to their values and their lifelong attempts to appear competent and adequate. There is enough ego strength ($C = 5$). He has the anxiety to keep him motivated (Q_4+) and the intelligence to make him a good patient ($B = 8$). Therapy would probably have to move in the direction of teaching him to bind his anxiety better, and to develop more effective ego defenses in general, particularly with regard to greater self-control and restraint.

PSYCHIATRIC EVALUATION SUMMARY:

Since a psychiatric summary is available, it is presented. The evaluation was done by a board-certified psychiatrist after the 16 PF evaluation was made:

" . . . In summary, Mr. Kenneth L. displays clinical evidence of immaturity. He shows considerable insecurity about himself and wants to blame this on his small stature. It is interesting that he describes his liking to fly airplanes as being due to the good feeling of looking down on others. Although he does not give the impression of being unreliable or irresponsible, it does appear that he tends to over-react to situations emotionally. He admits that he readily has a loss of temper if he feels that he is being taken advantage of in any way. As demonstrated by his having started many tasks without having completed them, I would feel that these personality characteristics would not lend themselves well for work as a sonar operator, and I suspect that he would not complete the training program if he embarked on it. The most appropriate diagnosis would be: personality disorder, passive-dependent type, moderate, with hysterical features."

FOLLOW-UP:

Mr. Kenneth L. was not hired, and all that we know about him subsequent to this is that he left the area. However, the case is a fascinating one, especially in the similarity between the 16 PF and the psychiatric evaluation. They differ in details, but both concluded that there were character problems, and emphasized great immaturity. It is these similarities that are gratifying to the clinician.

Case VIII: Mr. William L

A Suicide

PRESENTING PROBLEM:

We know very little about this man. He was 34 years old, and was an operating engineer for a steel rolling mill. Such mills are generally completely automatic, but it was his job to watch the operation of the automatic machines. The power used to roll steel is immense, and if the automatic controls fail, the machines can easily tear themselves apart. Further, there is the very real danger of personal injury when working around 6,000 horsepower motors that can go awry. The company for which Mr. William L. worked routinely administered the 16 PF to prospective employees at the outset. His profile was so unusual that the writers were asked to look it over. The report generated at that time follows. Subsequent to that time, after a period of about six months, Mr. William L. killed himself. He did not leave a suicide note, and little was known about his life from the time of testing until his death. The fact of the suicide was not known at the time of writing the 16 PF report.

IN-DEPTH INTERPRETATION:

A review of this man's 16 PF profile suggests an extremely guilt-laden, worried, and anxious person ($O = 9$) with low ego strength ($C = 4$). Further, he suffers from an unusually high degree of free-floating anxiety ($Q4$), and seems to have an overly strong sense of duty ($G = 7$, $O = 9$). In other words, not only is he high on group conformity (G) and conventional in his behavior, but he has an overly harsh, archaic superego, with much introjection of guilt. The latter is reflected in his very high score on O. He is seen as an unusually

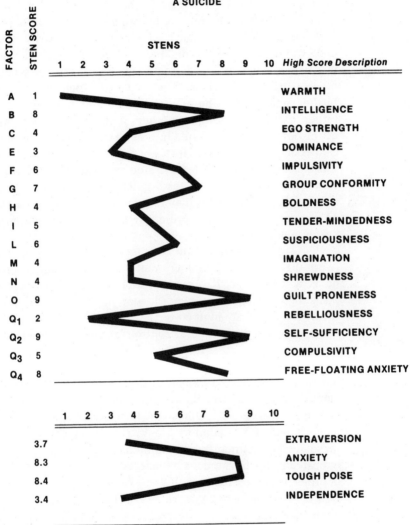

FIGURE 6-8
CASE VIII. MR. WILLIAM L.
A SUICIDE

FACTOR	STEN SCORE	High Score Description
A	1	WARMTH
B	8	INTELLIGENCE
C	4	EGO STRENGTH
E	3	DOMINANCE
F	6	IMPULSIVITY
G	7	GROUP CONFORMITY
H	4	BOLDNESS
I	5	TENDER-MINDEDNESS
L	6	SUSPICIOUSNESS
M	4	IMAGINATION
N	4	SHREWDNESS
O	9	GUILT PRONENESS
Q1	2	REBELLIOUSNESS
Q2	9	SELF-SUFFICIENCY
Q3	5	COMPULSIVITY
Q4	8	FREE-FLOATING ANXIETY

3.7	EXTRAVERSION
8.3	ANXIETY
8.4	TOUGH POISE
3.4	INDEPENDENCE

MD = 1

submissive person (E = 3). This is especially unusual in the light of his high intelligence (B = 8) and one wonders what events in his early life led him to be so humble. Also interesting is his minimal score of 1 on A; this indicates that he is unusually cool, aloof, and reserved. Frequently A— is associated with harsh parental relationships during childhood. He is shy and withdrawn, based on the extraversion factors just mentioned, namely, A—, H—, and Q_2+, and the low second-order extraversion factor. The unusually high score on O further indicates that he blames himself and is intropunitive, rather than acting out against others in his environment. Such acting out would be indicated by a more extraverted or hysterical personality structure. His Q_4 of 8 further suggests that he was concerned, tense, felt frustrated and irritable, and was in turmoil at the time of the testing. The second-order anxiety score of 8.3 also indicates that he is far more anxious on all the anxiety indicators than is ordinarily found in someone in his profession.

Further, the extremely low score of 1 on A (warmth) coupled with high Q_2 (self-sufficiency) suggests that he is a loner who has gotten little emotional support or pleasure from other people. Indeed, he moves away from them. His relatively high cortertia (tough poise) score shows that he has good intellectual controls and is capable of good work.

Another matter which should be considered has to do with the factors measuring anger on the 16 PF—E (dominance) and Q_1 (rebelliousness). On these, he gets scores of 3 and 2, respectively. Obviously, he tends to suppress angry feelings and is not comfortable in the direct expression of these feelings either through dominance or aggression, as indicated by his E. Nor does he markedly engage in displacing or projecting angry feelings (L = 6). At the same time, the low Q_1 shows that he doesn't get rid of his angry impulses through intellectual channels. The low Q_1 also shows him to be conservative and respectful of tradition. This combination of E— and Q_1—, coupled with high superego introjection (high O) provides the suggestion that this is a very conflicted, guilty man, terribly worried, and under immense stress. But he has few channels for getting rid of his anger; this is an unfortunate combination.

The MD score of 1 is also noteworthy. It is so low as to be an additional reflection of the way in which this person feels about himself and the task with which he's faced; he's direct and forthright in responding to these personality items. It's always surprising to see otherwise bright people, in jobs where a profile of this type would lead to further psychiatric examination, give such open profiles. We've seen it in military screening and in other situations. People in jobs like that often admit to headaches, dizziness, and other symptoms. It simply has to be regarded as a cry for help. Perhaps it shouldn't be surprising. After all, in psychometric testing anxiety may be expressed as a willingness to admit to common frailties. Apparently, if a person is under enormous stress, and is given an opportunity to relieve himself of some of it, he takes advantage of the opportunity and answers a great many items in a direction unfavorable to himself.

A diagnosis would be difficult to make. However, it's obvious that there is much anxiety and guilt. Our guess is that of an anxiety neurosis with strong depressive features. He is certainly a candidate for psychotherapy. However, as we've mentioned before, we don't regard the prognosis for permanently changing high anxiety with psychotherapy alone as very favorable. But depression and suffering can be reduced and he certainly needs help. There is potential in this man; he has good intelligence, and his ego strength (C) is not all that low.

FOLLOW-UP:

It is known that he killed himself after the 16 PF had been given, but we know little of the suicidal act itself.

It's instructive to view the profile in retrospect, with the knowledge that this man did in fact kill himself. We can now see many indications of suicide. We would expect to find high anxiety (Q_4), and it is there. In addition, we would expect to find high superego introjection, and that is there in immense quantity ($O = 9$). Worse, his G is also somewhat elevated. There is much superego, morality, and conventionality. Further, E and Q_1 are both low. He can't express his anger directly by confronting others, and he can't express it through intellectual channels. Thus, most of the outside pathways are gone, and there is little alternative but to turn it back on himself. It is worth noting that if L had also been high, dealing with anxious insecurity, we'd expect to find that the person is turning to alcohol, assuming O+ and Q4+ as well. But this man was apparently forced to simply sit there and take it, and he couldn't endure the pain.

Case IX: Mr. Edgar A. P.

A Paranoid Personality

PRESENTING PROBLEM:

We know little about this man, save that he is 23, and that he was diagnosed as a paranoid personality. He was initially seen by a psychiatrist as a result of his odd behavior. A 16 PF which had been administered two years before his psychiatric evaluation was available. The 16 PF interpretation, made without knowledge of the diagnosis, follows.

IN-DEPTH INTERPRETATION:

Mr. Edgar A. P. earns a score of 1 on Factors C (ego strength), H (boldness), and Q3 (ability to bind anxiety), and a score of 10 on O (guilt proneness), I (emotional sensitivity), and Q4 (free-floating anxiety), and the second-order anxiety score. Further, he makes a high score of 8 on L (suspiciousness or anxious insecurity). These scores, along with the 6 on E (dominance) and the 7 on Q1 (rebelliousness), indicate that this man is suffering from many sources of anxiety. They not only make him feel guilty and worried, but the L and E hint that he projects and displaces his angry feelings, in contrast to the intropunitive way in which an anxiety neurotic would ordinarily handle his angry feelings. The low MD (0) shows that he is not dissimulating in his replies to the items.

He is seen not only as highly anxious but also as highly introverted. This is shown by 3's on A (warmth) and F (impulsivity), a 1 on H (boldness), and a 7 on Q2 (self-sufficiency). The score of 1 on ego strength (C) is so low as to suggest that his ego defense organization is a patchwork quilt. He does not possess sufficient emotional stability to confront the trials and tribulations of everyday life. The I of 10 points to an extraordinary degree of emotional sensitivity and further

FIGURE 6-9
CASE IX. MR. EDGAR A. P.
A PARANOID PERSONALITY

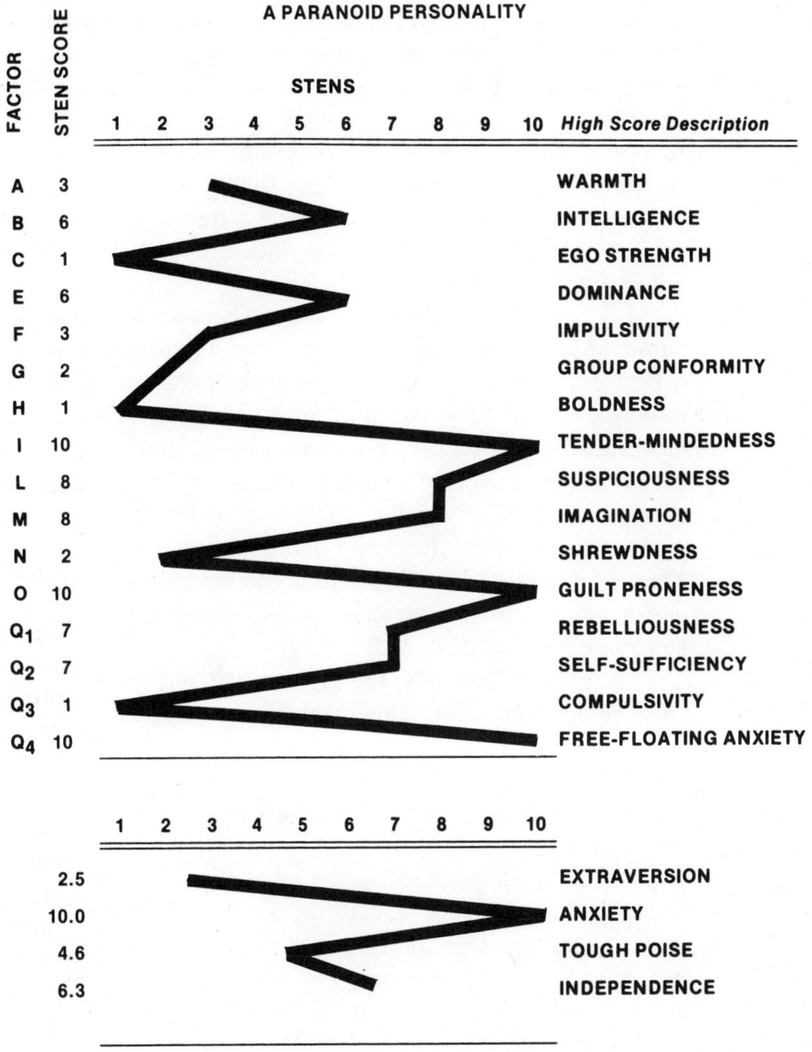
FACTOR
STEN SCORE
STENS
1 2 3 4 5 6 7 8 9 10
High Score Description
A 3 WARMTH
B 6 INTELLIGENCE
C 1 EGO STRENGTH
E 6 DOMINANCE
F 3 IMPULSIVITY
G 2 GROUP CONFORMITY
H 1 BOLDNESS
I 10 TENDER-MINDEDNESS
L 8 SUSPICIOUSNESS
M 8 IMAGINATION
N 2 SHREWDNESS
O 10 GUILT PRONENESS
Q_1 7 REBELLIOUSNESS
Q_2 7 SELF-SUFFICIENCY
Q_3 1 COMPULSIVITY
Q_4 10 FREE-FLOATING ANXIETY
1 2 3 4 5 6 7 8 9 10
2.5 EXTRAVERSION
10.0 ANXIETY
4.6 TOUGH POISE
6.3 INDEPENDENCE

MD = 0

reinforces what was said about the amount of pain, discomfort, guilt, and anxiety which he is suffering. For some reason, this high score on I is typical of persons suffering from paranoia in its various forms. The highly unusual score of 1 on H (shyness) emphasizes great dispositional timidity and the susceptibility to overwhelming anxiety described earlier. Coupled with the tendency to project, indicated by his high score of 8 on L (suspiciousness), the profile suggests that this is more than a severe neurosis. This is especially so in light of his great dispositional timidity (H—) coupled with L+ and Q_1+ (rebelliousness).

To recapitulate the reasons for a diagnosis of paranoid personality, note first that ego defenses are greatly overtaxed, as shown by the overwhelming anxiety. The pattern of the scores is strikingly unusual. Further, there is a 1 on dispositional timidity or shyness (H—), indicating strong hereditary, pathological factors entering into the situation. All of this, coupled with the highly introverted scores and problems with anger, implies a paranoid personality disorder. There is an almost complete inability to bind anxiety ($Q_3 = 1$) and severe identity problems. All of these taken together suggest a personality disorder.

Certainly, the high I of 10 and the low H of 1 must be accounted for. This combination suggests an overly strong identification with the mother and a poor identification with the father which could lead to sex role conflicts. In any case, the evidence is there to suggest strong identity problems ($Q_3 = 1$).

Masochistic aspects of the case are emphasized by the G of 2, which measures unconventionality, coupled with the O+, indicating a punitive conscience. The very low A and the similarly low second-order extraversion score clearly indicate a move away from other people. This is a person who takes his responsibilities seriously, even grimly ($F = 3$). And there is a naive quality about him ($N = 2$).

If this is indeed a case of paranoid personality, we must account for the low MD score, as we had to in the case of Mr. Richard M. Here, this can be done on the assumption that the person administering the test managed to obtain a remarkable degree of rapport and cooperation from the patient.

The thing that strikes us about this profile, in addition to what has already been mentioned, is the very high I (emotional sensitivity). Psychologists and psychiatrists often obtain I scores this high (10), for being aware of the feelings that they and other people have is their business. But it is unusual in other people. It reflects an exquisite, extraordinary sensitivity to pain and vulnerability to id impulses. It's just the thing needed by a good paranoid to prolong his resentment.

FOLLOW-UP:

The odd thing about Mr. Edgar A. P. is that he didn't wind up as a social liability, as was initially feared. Since he was an exceptionally handsome young man and was interested in the theatre, he was able to join a theatrical company and make a good living by playing bit parts and working as a stage hand. But there has been little improvement in the mistrust with which he regards other persons.

Case X: Mr. John P.

A Verified Psychomatic Disorder

PRESENTING PROBLEM:

This man, 41, was formerly an executive in a large company. He had been in a position involving enormous tension, and was eventually retired from the company because of a series of migraine headaches, disabling him for the job. The headaches had been occurring for years, and in the past he had consulted his family doctor and a neurologist about them. The examinations were completely negative, and the diagnosis made was that of tension headaches. The patient had refused to take a prescription for tranquilizers which were prescribed in the hope of alleviating the headaches, since he denied that he had psychological problems of any kind. In the last few weeks before the testing, he did begin taking tranquilizers for a recently developed insomnia. The following interpretation was written with knowledge only of the patient's age and the fact that health problems made it necessary for him to retire from his position.

IN-DEPTH INTERPRETATION:

The most striking thing about the profile is the minimum score possible on the ability to bind anxiety, or Q_3,

FIGURE 6-10
CASE X. MR. JOHN P.
A VERIFIED PSYCHOSOMATIC DISORDER

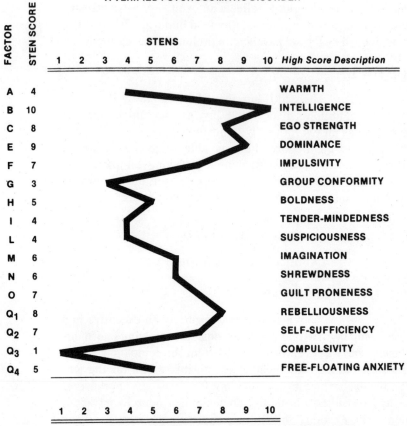

FACTOR	STEN SCORE		High Score Description
A	4		WARMTH
B	10		INTELLIGENCE
C	8		EGO STRENGTH
E	9		DOMINANCE
F	7		IMPULSIVITY
G	3		GROUP CONFORMITY
H	5		BOLDNESS
I	4		TENDER-MINDEDNESS
L	4		SUSPICIOUSNESS
M	6		IMAGINATION
N	6		SHREWDNESS
O	7		GUILT PRONENESS
Q_1	8		REBELLIOUSNESS
Q_2	7		SELF-SUFFICIENCY
Q_3	1		COMPULSIVITY
Q_4	5		FREE-FLOATING ANXIETY

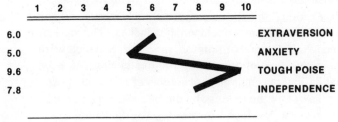

		High Score Description
6.0		EXTRAVERSION
5.0		ANXIETY
9.6		TOUGH POISE
7.8		INDEPENDENCE

MD = 8

130

of 1. Stice has termed Q3 the "gyroscopic" factor in personality, according to the 16 PF *Handbook* (Cattell et al., 1970, p. 107). It is related to identification in the sense that a successfully introjected identity consists largely of the acquisition of a set of habits demanded by a job. Q3— indicates that such introjection has not occurred. Low Q3 can point to other evidence of unresolved problems in the profile, especially anxiety, since Q3 is on the second-order anxiety factor. But an inspection of the primary anxiety factor scores shows that only on O, where he earned a score of 7 (guilt proneness), is this hypothesis warranted. Q4, for example, falls within the average range. Factor O has to do with introjected superego, specifically superego-generated anxiety, and consequently implies guilt feelings and chronic worrying. On the other hand, Q4 measures id tension or free-floating anxiety, and is more directly related to the feelings of tension generated by a lack of psychological equilibrium or low ego strength. His G of 3 is also low. As we said in Chapter 4, we disagree somewhat with Professor Cattell in his identification of Factor G as being the primary measure of effective superego. True, G is in many cases a measure of conscience, but it is only one of several. Factor O, which we believe measures superego-generated guilt or anxiety, is to our mind a much more effective measure. G+ indicates conventionality, with emphasis on external appearances rather than on the more crucial issue of having successfully introjected parental teachings and sanctions. A sociopath, then, could well be someone at least average or high on G, who gives the appearance of being conventional, but who has less than average superego introjection (O—).

In the present case the G of 3 suggests low group conformity, often interpreted by others as unconventionality, while actually Mr. John P. tends to feel quite guilty and worries excessively (O+). As mentioned in Case VI, the pattern of G— and O+ is often seen in neurotic patients.

Returning to the profile, we see an MD score of 8. This suggests that the anxiety scores may be underestimates. The only primaries, under the influence of the MD, in which anxiety is prominent are Q3— and O+. There is evidence of difficulty with anger in the E (dominance) of 9 and the Q1 (rebelliousness) of 8. This pattern has already appeared in several cases previously encountered. E measures how pushy a person is and how likely he is to confront others directly. Q1 expresses hostility handled through more covert means. In a person with a B of 10, anger is even more likely to be the problem, since he possesses the necessary intelligence to express his hostility effectively. The low Q3 might raise the problem of whether he has the compulsivity to do this, however. Many neurotics are unable to use their talents constructively, and, instead, dissipate their energies. Further, the high F of 7 combined with the L of 4 suggests an impulsive, trusting, immature person.

The pattern on the extraversion factors is unusual. He is somewhat low on A (warmth) and high on Q2 (self-sufficiency); both indicate introversion. At the same time he is F+ (impulsive) and average on H (boldness).

In this case we see again, as in several previous cases, A— and I—, accompanied by an average or low M. This is the pattern felt to be especially vulnerable to the development of psychosomatic symptoms under stress. A, I, and M go together to make up the second-order factor of cortertia or tough poise, often indicative of such problems, especially when there is evidence of undue anxiety and anger.

With regard to diagnosis, the major psychodynamics center around much anger and guilt with virtually no ability to bind anxiety. There is also a tendency toward a hardboiled approach to life. Typically such psychodynamics are seen in the etiology of psychosomatic reactions. The prognosis depends on the source of the stress—his job, his marriage, and other circumstances. But his high intelligence shows that he has the potential to handle his problems better. This is a positive sign for psychotherapy. Further, his age is no handicap, and he has enough anxiety to motivate him. Essentially, we see a man with problems with id impulses, much immaturity, an inability to bind anxiety, and a lack of emotional sensitivity.

FOLLOW-UP:

Mr. John P. obtained a job similar to his previous one with another company, and the headaches persisted. He did not enter psychotherapy, feeling that it would be too "sissified." It is presumed that the psychosomatic symptoms will persist, but it appears that he can live with them, probably at great cost to his health.

Case XI: The A.'s

A Married Couple in Psychotherapy

PRESENTING PROBLEM:

Mrs. A. is in her late 20's, and her husband, an attorney, is a year older. They have two children, a boy and a girl. Mrs. A. sought supportive treatment from a psychotherapist on the recommendation of her husband's analyst. As part of the initial interview her prospective therapist administered the 16 PF, which resulted in the interpretation which follows. The therapist expressed particular concern about Mrs. A.'s suitability for treatment and also wanted to know whether there was enough stability in the marriage to make psychotherapy feasible. Both profiles are shown in Figure 6-11.

IN-DEPTH INTERPRETATIONS:

Mrs. A.

She has an MD score of only 2, indicating no problem with Motivational Distortion. This sort of low score is characteristic of patients presenting themselves for psychotherapy. Extreme scores occur on B+, F—, G—, and Q3—. The 10 on B (intelligence) suggests that she is exceptionally bright. The unusually low score of 1 on F (impulsivity) is especially interesting. It shows her to be a glum, serious, sober person, almost totally lacking in spontaneity, or "surgency," as Cattell calls it. She lacks enthusiasm and cheerfulness. An F this low is often a derivative of parents who impose heavy expectations on their children at à very early age and provide them with little dependency gratification. Such children frequently lack the ability to enjoy life, experience only limited id gratification, and are overly conscientious.

Usually a low F and a low G (group conformity) are not found together, since, on the surface, they would seem to point to opposite things; but the combination is present on Mrs. A.'s profile. However, we notice that the very low score on group conformity (G) is accompanied by a high score of 9 on M (imagination), and this makes better sense. Factor M has been nicknamed the "Walter Mitty" factor; a high M indicates someone who tends to dissociate and has an

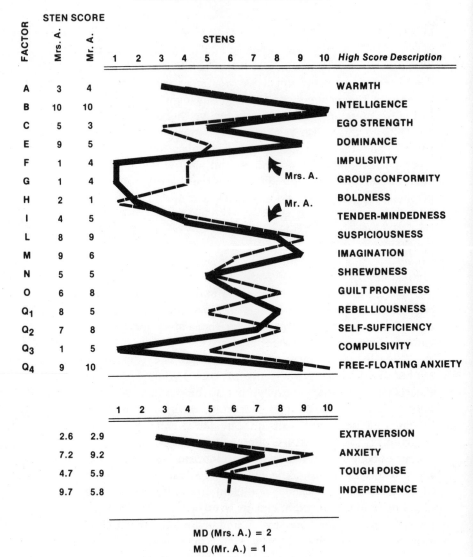

FIGURE 6-11
CASE XI. THE A.'s
A MARRIED COUPLE IN PSYCHOTHERAPY

STEN SCORE

FACTOR	Mrs. A.	Mr. A.	High Score Description
A	3	4	WARMTH
B	10	10	INTELLIGENCE
C	5	3	EGO STRENGTH
E	9	5	DOMINANCE
F	1	4	IMPULSIVITY
G	1	4	GROUP CONFORMITY
H	2	1	BOLDNESS
I	4	5	TENDER-MINDEDNESS
L	8	9	SUSPICIOUSNESS
M	9	6	IMAGINATION
N	5	5	SHREWDNESS
O	6	8	GUILT PRONENESS
Q_1	8	5	REBELLIOUSNESS
Q_2	7	8	SELF-SUFFICIENCY
Q_3	1	5	COMPULSIVITY
Q_4	9	10	FREE-FLOATING ANXIETY

	2.6	2.9	EXTRAVERSION
	7.2	9.2	ANXIETY
	4.7	5.9	TOUGH POISE
	9.7	5.8	INDEPENDENCE

MD (Mrs. A.) = 2
MD (Mr. A.) = 1

134

active fantasy life. M has been found to be related to creativity. Consequently, low G and high M frequently accompany one another.

The very low F leads us to expect at least average superego introjection. With this in mind we look at O, and discover that it is 6, just high average. This is rather odd, for O is another superego indicator. But we must remember that the absolute magnitude of the scores must be looked at in the light of the context in which they occur. An extremely low F of 1 tempers the meaning of an O of 6. In this case, with the low F, we take the 6 on O as being more significant than we would otherwise.

The score of 1 on Q_3 (low ability to bind anxiety or compulsivity) indicates that she is terribly lax and uncertain. It also points to an identity problem, and this, indeed, may be the major reason that she's seeking treatment. It is hard to see her as being happy or satisfied with her role in life. The combination of B+ and Q_3- is also rare. One wonders if there is currently any way that this young woman can use her substantial intellectual power constructively. This idea is further supported by the low G. G+ and Q_3+ have been found to go together on the second-order factor of compulsivity-vs.-sociopathy. Evidence is building that Mrs. A. has few effective defenses against anxiety.

Looking at the second-order anxiety score of 7.2 and the Q_4 (free-floating anxiety) of 9, we can be sure of the presence of much anxiety, probably accompanied by irritability, feelings of frustration, and insomnia. If the anxiety-binding function of Q_3+ were operating in this case, we would not expect to see such a high degree of anxiety. Almost all the other components of the second-order anxiety factor are also up. L, Q_3, and Q_4 are all in the expected direction, and we have hypothesized that the O of 6 should, perhaps, be taken as being more deviant than it appears. This means that the only atypical anxiety component is C (ego strength), where the score is 5, or average. We regard this as a positive factor, suggesting that she could improve with therapy. We must be aware that the high score on anxiety could well be inflated by the tendency of patients presenting themselves for psychotherapy to look as bad as possible. However, we should be concerned by the L (suspiciousness) of 8. This suggests heavy use of projection, and with the E (dominance) of 9, she evidently has severe problems in coping with her angry feelings. The Q_1 (rebelliousness) is also elevated, suggesting critical, castrating tendencies on her part which reinforces our speculations about her problems with handling angry feelings. Her Q_1+ also serves as an outlet for some of her anger and in all likelihood helps her defend against depression.

Her husband probably finds her extremely difficult and unrewarding to live with because her intense anger, criticalness and castration tendencies surely make him unduly uncomfortable.

In a complicated case of this kind we cannot be certain of a diagnosis, but we would hazard the guess of a severe anxiety neurosis with strong depressive features. There is little question that psychotherapy should be begun.

Mr. A.

We can't help but wonder about the dynamics of a man who is married to a woman with such a heavy burden of problems. He's candid (MD $=$ 1) and bright (B+), just as she is. Also, he suffers from extraordinarily high free-floating anxiety ($Q_4 =$ 10). Thus far they're very similar; however, he is just average on E (dominance) and Q_1 (rebelliousness), indicating that he has a lot less anger than his wife. But his L of 9 implies that he is very uncomfortable and has much difficulty in handling his angry feelings which he typically deals with through displacement and projection. And, like her, he is extremely anxious ($Q_4 =$ 10) and dispositionally timid (H $=$ 1); neither of them is able to take risks. Like her, there is little warmth in his personality functioning (A $=$ 4) and a similar tendency toward introversion (2.9). He suffers more from guilt than she does (O+). We are particularly concerned about his low score on ego strength (C—) and his great timidity (H—). However, he does have very high intelligence and far fewer identity problems than she does, which suggests that at least he derives some satisfaction from his job as an attorney.

The Marriage:

Putting the two profiles together, we can expect that the family climate is not a happy one. We can only guess at the effect such a climate has on the children, since both parents are anxious, irritable, glum, even depressive, and the mother particularly hostile and ungiving. Perhaps this is exactly the kind of family environment the two of them grew up in, and they have unfortunately been helpless to do anything about it so far but reproduce their own childhood milieu.

We've observed over the years that older children seem to catch most of the flak from the parents, and we would hazard the guess that the son was making a particularly perilous adjustment, and had a great number of fears, including persistent nightmares. This is not a giving couple, nor a happy marriage, and the children must surely be feeling the effects of living with highly anxious, demanding, and angry parents, who have very little warmth or dependency gratification to offer anyone.

FOLLOW-UP:

The A.'s are still together, and still in analysis. This might be expected, since both of them have chronic personality problems and strong sado-masochistic needs which are difficult to change. They apparently have sufficiently complementary needs to continue trying to work things out. But it would be difficult to imagine that they have a happy marriage or that the family has much fun together.

Case XII: Ms. X. Y.

A Case of Transsexuality

Ms. X. Y. is included as an instance of a truly remarkable case. Unfortunately, the 16 PF did not succeed in picking up her precise problem, but the case remains spectacular.

PRESENTING PROBLEM:

The patient was a 32-year-old man, who is now legally a woman. Beyond the fact that her fitness for her job was questioned after the sex change operation, we elect not to discuss the details of the case, to protect her identity. However, we should mention that she was given the 16 PF as part of a test battery about two years after surgery. This interpretation was written with knowledge about the case. We have tried again and again to highlight the psychodynamics that point to her basic problem, but invariably we were unsuccessful.

IN-DEPTH INTERPRETATION:

Like most persons in her profession, she was somewhat high on cortertia (6.6). All the anxiety scores are average or not remarkable. This might imply that there is no problem with anxiety, but the MD is 10, indicating that she was putting her best foot forward. This attitude on her part is understandable, since she was being evaluated pursuant to establishing her suitability for a job which she wanted.

She has high intelligence (B = 8). We also see the combination of E+ (dominance) and Q_1+ (rebelliousness), commented on in previous cases as indicating aggression and anger. She is a bit introverted (extraversion = 4.8), her scores on A (warmth) and F (impulsivity) of 4, and the Q_2 (self-sufficiency) of 7 all point in that direction.

Surprisingly, she is portrayed as a tough, practical person who is emotionally insensitive (I = 4). It seems paradoxical, in view of her problem, that she is I—, although her history supports the idea that she could have an interest pattern that is typically "masculine," of the sort associated with an interest in mechanical things. She is somewhat below average in superego introjection (O = 4), although her group conformity is high (G = 7), as is her attitude toward responsibility (F = 4, $Q_3 = 8$), and her ability to bind anxiety. In short, she is more compulsive than sociopathic, and she seems to have introjected a suitable ego ideal!

Frequently, H and I are factors on the 16 PF which give clues about the person's identification with her parents, and they should be of help here. High H frequently suggests a love of adventure usually associated with a strongly "masculine" interest pattern. Her H of 6 is not contradictory of an identification with the father, but neither is it strongly supportive. However, the I (emotional sensitivity) of 4 hints that a "masculine" identity has been introjected.[2] Other clues of sex role identification may occasionally be gleaned from the factors dealing with superego controls, namely, F, G, O, and Q_3. Even here, though, it is difficult to know which of these

---

[2]This interpretation needs to be qualified, since identification with a father figure who is high on I can be reflected in a high I in the son.

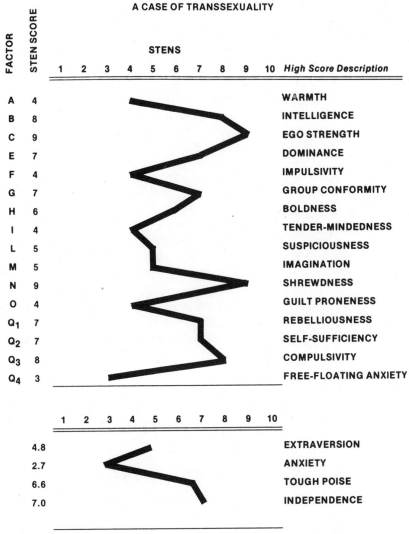

FIGURE 6-12
CASE XII. MS. X. Y.
A CASE OF TRANSSEXUALITY

FACTOR	STEN SCORE		High Score Description
A	4		WARMTH
B	8		INTELLIGENCE
C	9		EGO STRENGTH
E	7		DOMINANCE
F	4		IMPULSIVITY
G	7		GROUP CONFORMITY
H	6		BOLDNESS
I	4		TENDER-MINDEDNESS
L	5		SUSPICIOUSNESS
M	5		IMAGINATION
N	9		SHREWDNESS
O	4		GUILT PRONENESS
Q_1	7		REBELLIOUSNESS
Q_2	7		SELF-SUFFICIENCY
Q_3	8		COMPULSIVITY
Q_4	3		FREE-FLOATING ANXIETY

4.8	EXTRAVERSION
2.7	ANXIETY
6.6	TOUGH POISE
7.0	INDEPENDENCE

MD = 10

139

has been influenced by a particular parent if you don't have direct knowledge of the parents' 16 PF profiles.

In summary, we must suspect the validity of the anxiety scores, and, indeed, of the whole profile because of the high MD. We have previously emphasized that a high ego strength score (C = 9) must be tempered when accompanied by a high MD. Nevertheless, it is apparent that the 16 PF profile contains little or no evidence of high anxiety, or of any other major problem except for anger (E and Q_1 = 7). Certainly, the transsexuality does not appear prominent in the profile. Moreover, if O had been high, we could speculate that her anger was turned back on herself rather than being displaced, since L is 5 and she is introversive. But it isn't.

FOLLOW-UP:

After a long legal battle, Ms. X. Y. won the right to keep her job, but she had grown so weary of the legal process that she was already well established in another occupation more to her liking.

Perhaps we are expecting too much from the 16 PF in this instance since the record shows she was given three different diagnoses by highly qualified and experienced medical specialists. It would have been nice if a 16 PF profile, given prior to the surgery, had been obtained.

Case XIII: Mr. Harry B.

A Man with High Cortertia

PRESENTING PROBLEM:

Mr. Harry B. was the radio operator on a large ship which foundered in a storm in the Atlantic with substantial loss of life. There was considerable question as to his culpability in this disaster, although the maritime courts could draw no precise conclusion in the matter. The 16 PF had been administered several years earlier as part of a routine pre-employment screening program.

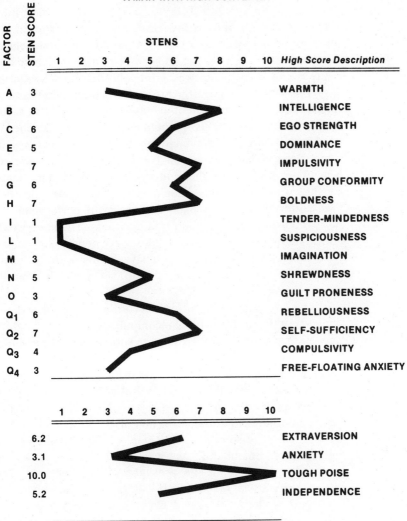

FIGURE 6-13
CASE XIII. MR. HARRY B.
A MAN WITH HIGH CORTERTIA

FACTOR	STEN SCORE	High Score Description
A	3	WARMTH
B	8	INTELLIGENCE
C	6	EGO STRENGTH
E	5	DOMINANCE
F	7	IMPULSIVITY
G	6	GROUP CONFORMITY
H	7	BOLDNESS
I	1	TENDER-MINDEDNESS
L	1	SUSPICIOUSNESS
M	3	IMAGINATION
N	5	SHREWDNESS
O	3	GUILT PRONENESS
Q_1	6	REBELLIOUSNESS
Q_2	7	SELF-SUFFICIENCY
Q_3	4	COMPULSIVITY
Q_4	3	FREE-FLOATING ANXIETY

6.2		EXTRAVERSION
3.1		ANXIETY
10.0		TOUGH POISE
5.2		INDEPENDENCE

MD = 7

141

IN-DEPTH INTERPRETATION:

His 16 PF profile shows a somewhat higher MD score than average (MD = 7). The most striking thing about the profile is the extreme score on the second-order factor of cortertia (tough poise) of 10. This can clearly be seen in its primaries, A—, I—, and M—. A second-order factor descriptive of this construct was originally identified by Cattell (1957) on which A (warmth), I (emotional sensitivity), and M (imagination) had prominent negative loadings. This factor was called "cortertia-vs.-pathemia." Pathemia implies a sentimental, largely emotionally based response tendency. In comparison, someone high on cortertia arrives at decisions largely on the basis of the evidence rather than sentimental considerations. Decisions made by Sherlock Holmes illustrate high cortertia. It shows itself in successful performance in tasks requiring accurate and rapid decisions. Thus, we would anticipate that Mr. Harry B. would be very good in such situations if he possessed the compulsive habits with sufficient intelligence and independent self-sufficiency which typically accompany cortertia.

Apart from high cortertia, the most striking thing about the profile is his Q_3 (compulsivity) of only 4, which is not high enough for someone in the sort of job that he holds, even though his intelligence is high (B = 8). Q_3 measures "disciplined accuracy," as we call it; it's similar to compulsivity. Thus, even though Harry B. has much potential for his kind of work, unfortunately, he does not have the compulsive habits to actualize his potential.

A somewhat low Q_3 is usually accompanied by high anxiety. But in this case we have C+, L—, O—, and Q_4—, all contradicting the presence of high anxiety. The second-order anxiety factor itself is only 3.1. What is happening to his anxiety? We could hypothesize the possibility of psychosomatic symptoms, and they could have an anxiety-binding effect in this instance which would help to explain the occurrence of Q_3— accompanied by low levels of anxiety from other sources.

But the remainder of the profile shows immaturity and impulsivity (F = 7) with low dispositional timidity (H = 7). Both reinforce the idea of a highly masculine ego-ideal as well as a propensity for "acting-out" behavior.

Because of this pattern, it is essential to review the superego factors, F, G, Q3, and O. He is about average on conventionality (G), somewhat immature (F), and does not suffer much guilt and worry (O = 3). And he is far from rigidly adhering to a socially approved value system (Q3 = 4). We can thus expect it is more likely for him to experience difficulties in impulse control and resort to acting-out behavior rather than develop psychosomatic symptoms.

In sum, he is an extremely practical, tough-minded person of above average intelligence who is low on disciplined accuracy. One must wonder about his very low scores on anxiety. Because of the limited evidence of anxiety in an impulsive, immature man with a highly masculine ego ideal (H = 7, I = 1) and a weak introjected superego (O = 3), we might hazard the diagnosis of a personality disorder. Certainly, questions are raised concerning his job suitability.

FOLLOW-UP:

The nature of our contact with Mr. Harry B. was such that information was difficult to find about his subsequent life. However, we do know that he was not immediately rehired by another ship line. And, after a maritime hearing of such notoriety, it is likely that he had difficulty in obtaining future employment in the same line of work.

Case XIV: Mr. Paul B.

A Situational Reaction

PRESENTING PROBLEM:

Mr. Paul B. is a 27-year-old married man, with one child, on whom we have two 16 PF profiles. At the time of the second testing he was separated from his wife and was living with another woman. However, he was in great turmoil over the decision of whether to return to his wife and family. His marital conflicts culminated in his committing himself to a psychiatric ward for a period of a week, and then leaving. Since that time he has consulted a psychiatrist and has been taking heavy dosages of tranquilizers.

He works as an air traffic controller for a government agency, guiding large airliners to and from landings and takeoffs at major airports. Since this is a terribly important job, the regulations do not permit persons on tranquilizers to perform these duties. The first report (on the second profile) was written as part of an evaluation of his fitness to return to duty.

IN-DEPTH INTERPRETATION OF THE SECOND PROFILE:

Paul B. earned a 10 on F (impulsivity) and H (boldness), and 1 on G (group conformity) and Q_2 (self-sufficiency). The MD of 8 is high enough to suggest that he was faking a bit in his efforts to be returned to his job.

The score of 9.7 on extraversion indicates he is extremely outgoing and perhaps that he has an hysterical personality structure. The 9 on A (warmth) suggests a strong need to interact with others; this is accompanied by much impulsivity and immaturity ($F = 10$), indicating a great lack of restraint. Moreover, his H of 10 implies boldness and much interest in the opposite sex. Maximum scores on F and H make one wonder about the wisdom of putting this person in a situation involving other people's lives, since he may well be careless and impulsive. The Q_2 of 1 is very low; he probably requires more interaction with other people as well as dependency gratification from them than would be optimal in his job.

All of the anxiety indicators are low, with the exception of Q_3. Even the second-order score itself is only 2.6. With the MD of 8, we must question the validity of these scores. The low group conformity score (G) accompanied by F+, O—, and Q_3— raises questions about the adequacy of his superego; he is especially vulnerable to temptation. What is depicted here is a character problem in a highly impulsive, immature, and dependent person who can be expected to act out his conflicts. Obviously, his personality problems contraindicate a return to his demanding and responsible job.

IN-DEPTH INTERPRETATION OF THE FIRST PROFILE:

He had also been tested earlier as part of a routine testing program of all controller applicants. On this profile his MD score of 5 was about average, but he again made near the maximum score on extraversion. He is depicted

FIGURE 6-14
CASE XIV. MR. PAUL B.
A SITUATIONAL REACTION

FACTOR	1st Testing	2nd Testing	High Score Description
A	10	9	WARMTH
B	8	5	INTELLIGENCE
C	3	8	EGO STRENGTH
E	5	6	DOMINANCE
F	9	10	IMPULSIVITY
G	5	1	GROUP CONFORMITY
H	9	10	BOLDNESS
I	8	8	TENDER-MINDEDNESS
L	6	4	SUSPICIOUSNESS
M	4	4	IMAGINATION
N	5	6	SHREWDNESS
O	4	2	GUILT PRONENESS
Q_1	3	5	REBELLIOUSNESS
Q_2	3	1	SELF-SUFFICIENCY
Q_3	4	4	COMPULSIVITY
Q_4	7	3	FREE-FLOATING ANXIETY

9.0	9.7		EXTRAVERSION
6.5	2.6		ANXIETY
2.9	4.5		TOUGH POISE
4.2	5.4		INDEPENDENCE

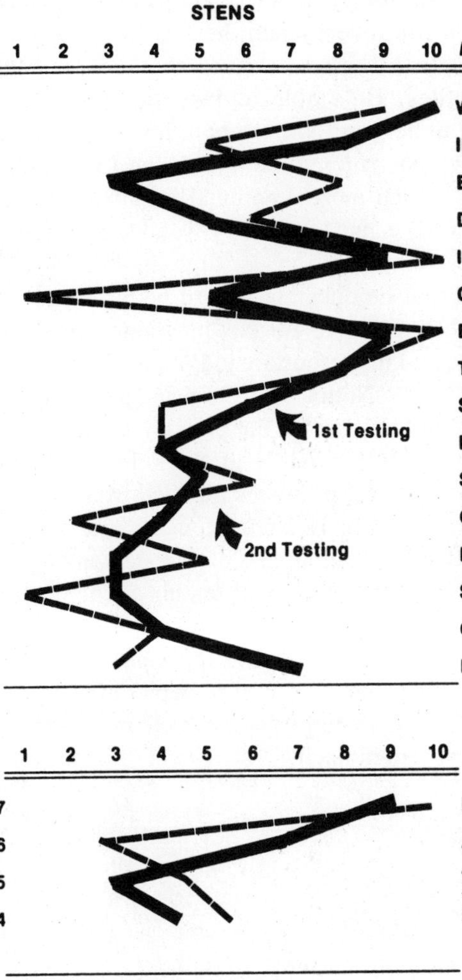

MD (1st Testing) = 5
MD (2nd Testing) = 8

145

as an outgoing person (A = 10) with strong dependency needs (Q_2 = 3), who is immature, impulsive (F = 9), and a high risk taker (H = 9).

On the anxiety factors, the ego strength score (C) of 3 is very low; notice how he has raised this score to an 8 in the second administration. The L of 6 (anxious insecurity) is high for a controller; again, he has lowered this score in the second testing. Notice, however, that the Q_3 of 4 is the same in both profiles. He's able to fake the more obvious anxiety factors, but he won't kid us about his lack of compulsivity; it's obviously ego-syntonic. Similarly, the I in both cases is 8; he admits to much more emotional sensitivity than the average controller. We must certainly wonder about his functioning efficiency on the job. F is high in both profiles, and it's apparent that he does not regard being happy-go-lucky as an undesirable trait. All in all, questions are raised about his immature and inappropriate judgment.

Notice that the principal differences between the two profiles occur on the primary anxiety factors. Clearly, Motivational Distortion is at work here. Nevertheless, the potential character problems gleaned from the high scores on both testings on F, H, and I demonstrate that, even when a subject is faking, glimpses of his personality structure can come through. On the initial testing he depicted himself as a conventional person, average with regard to group conformity. However, on the second testing, even when he was denying anxiety, he was not reluctant to depict himself as a low group conformer and as impulsive, which may well be congruent with his view of himself.

FOLLOW-UP:

Interestingly enough, there was disagreement between the 16 PF, the psychiatric evaluation, and the psychological evaluation. The psychiatrist felt that the diagnosis was a situational reaction, while the psychologist diagnosed it as a case of anxiety neurosis complicated by character problems. The 16 PF concurred with the latter, at least with regard to the character problems. In any event, Mr. Paul B. was not reassigned to his previous duties, although given a less responsible job. He returned to his wife, but in view of his personality programming, it seems likely he will continue to act out.

Case XV: Mrs. Alice W.

A Well-Adjusted Professional

PRESENTING PROBLEM:

Mrs. Alice W. is a 39-year-old woman with no children. She works full time as a nurse in a pediatric ward. She has been married for ten years, and has been gainfully employed all of her adult life. She took the 16 PF on a volunteer basis as a matter of interest while enrolled in a course on psychological testing.

IN-DEPTH INTERPRETATION:

A review of her profile makes us ask, "Where's her anger and what does she do with her angry feelings?" Although she gets the highest score possible on B (intelligence), her E (dominance) is only 4. This is an odd combination, since B+ and E+ are frequently found together. It makes us wonder what circumstance extinguished her aggressive behavior. This is particularly so in light of her high H of 8 (boldness). Moreover, her Q_1 of 4 is also below average and implies respect for tradition and conservatism rather than critical, rebellious tendencies which frequently accompany B+ and H+.

The second-order anxiety score of 2.9 is well below average. This is reflected in the primaries for this factor: C+ (ego strength), average L (suspiciousness), and below average O (guilt proneness). Her Q_3 of 8 indicates good ability to bind anxiety, and there is little free-floating anxiety ($Q_4 = 3$).

The second-order extraversion score of 3.5 suggests that she is not outgoing. Again, with the exception of the high H (boldness), the primaries bear this out: A = 4 (warmth), F = 2 (responsibility), and $Q_2 = 8$ (self-sufficiency). This is another unusual state of affairs, since H+ usually accompanies A+, F+, and Q_2—.

What about superego problems in this lady with so few signs of anxiety? Does she show character problems or sociopathic trends? Consider the G of 5 (group conformity), the F of 2 (responsibility), the O of 3 (guilt proneness), and the Q_3 of 8 (disciplined). We must conclude that

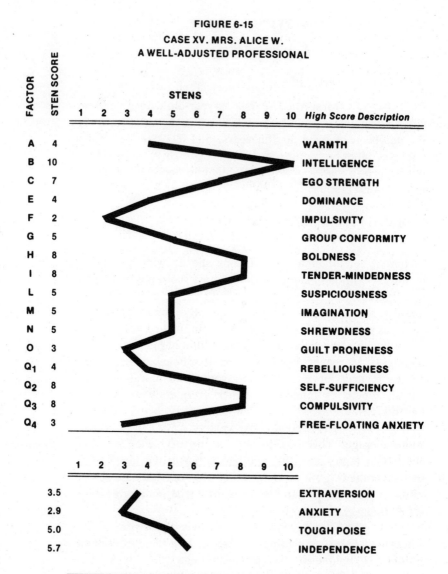

FIGURE 6-15
CASE XV. MRS. ALICE W.
A WELL-ADJUSTED PROFESSIONAL

FACTOR	STEN SCORE		High Score Description
A	4		WARMTH
B	10		INTELLIGENCE
C	7		EGO STRENGTH
E	4		DOMINANCE
F	2		IMPULSIVITY
G	5		GROUP CONFORMITY
H	8		BOLDNESS
I	8		TENDER-MINDEDNESS
L	5		SUSPICIOUSNESS
M	5		IMAGINATION
N	5		SHREWDNESS
O	3		GUILT PRONENESS
Q_1	4		REBELLIOUSNESS
Q_2	8		SELF-SUFFICIENCY
Q_3	8		COMPULSIVITY
Q_4	3		FREE-FLOATING ANXIETY

3.5		EXTRAVERSION
2.9		ANXIETY
5.0		TOUGH POISE
5.7		INDEPENDENCE

MD = 2

148

she shows few, if any, control problems in this area. In fact, if anything, considering what was said earlier about her apparent problem with anger (E—, Q_1—), she shows too much id restraint rather than too little, even though she is O—.

Finally, one wonders about why she got a below average score on A (warmth) and about her strong sense of responsibility previously discussed. As we have so frequently mentioned in these cases, such low scores are typically related to generally unfavorable early childhood family circumstances. It appears that demanding parents who place too great burdens on their children at early ages often wind up with offspring like this.

The Q_2 (self-sufficiency) of 8, in the context of B+ and Q_3+, also merits comment, since it implies excellent work habits in a practical (M = 5) but emotionally sensitive person (I = 8) who probably relates well to patients, and is capable of great empathy with them (I+). In effect, she is particularly well sublimated, has an effective network of ego defenses (C+, Q_3+), and shows few signs of frustration or undischarged id tension (Q_4—).

FOLLOW-UP:

An interview and her life history questionnaire revealed that both her parents died in an auto accident while she was still a child, and that she was raised by her widowed grandmother from that point on. She reported that she had always done well in school, and never had difficulty making good grades, even in college. She's always been very interested in civic affairs, and has remained active in a number of community organizations aimed at helping the less fortunate, in addition to her full-time job as chief ward nurse. She related that she and her husband, a policeman, get along well and enjoy their life together. They are particularly active in tennis and golf, and are fortunate to live in a climate which permits such activities year round.

Mrs. Alice W., thus, is an excellent example of a 16 PF from a normal, albeit not perfect, person.

APPENDIX A

Scoring the Supplementary Scales

As mentioned in Chapter 1, the writers have developed several scales to supplement the scales of the 16 PF. We routinely score these scales, even though they are not part of the scoring package provided by IPAT. You will find them frequently referred to in our case histories, provided that the cases are recent. We shall briefly describe the rationale behind these scales and the scoring procedure. Note that these scales are intended *only* for Form A.

The Motivational Distortion Scale

The "Motivational Distortion" (MD) scale, or "Faking Good" scale, as it could be called, was developed by having a group of 45 subjects answer the 16 PF in such a fashion as to provide the most favorable picture of themselves. The items were selected by comparing these answer sheets with a group of 283 normally answered protocols (Winder, O'Dell, & Karson, 1975). Items differentiating between the groups were selected, and the direction of their scoring is shown in Table A-1. These items were cross validated on another group of 37 persons, and a further cross-validation study has been done (Irvine, Gendreau, & O'Dell, in press). The cross-validation results have been most favorable. In

TABLE A-1

ITEMS ON THE MD AND FAKING BAD SCALES

MD		Faking Bad	
Item #	Direction	Item #	Direction
7	c	14	a
24	c	38	a
61	c	42	c
62	a	51	b
81	a	52	c
97	a	55	c
111	a	68	c
114	c	80	a
123	c	89	c
130	a	117	a
133	c	119	a
149	c	123	a
173	a	143	a
174	c	176	c
184	a	182	c

Source: Winder, O'Dell, & Karson (1975). Copyright 1975 by the Society for Personality Assessment, Inc. Reprinted by permission.

general, if one uses a cutting score of 6, one will pick up 85% of those faking good, while selecting out only 10% of those who had answered honestly. The accuracy increases with higher cutting scores. This obviously is not perfect selection, but the scales are invaluable in making a clinical decision about a dubious record.

Scoring is quite simple. It is easy to make up a little scoring key out of a 16 PF answer sheet of the type that one is using. You need only mark the items included on the scale in the direction of scoring indicated, and punch them out.[1] Then one has a scoring key. One point is counted for each alternative marked by the testee in the direction described in Table A-1.

---

[1] A handy punch for making up keys like this can be made from one of those little 25¢ paper punches found in bookstores. Break off the bottom plate of the punch, and take out the round punch part. By taping the bottom plate against a window, keys can easily be punched out.

The Faking Bad Scale

The Faking Bad scale was made up by having subjects fake the 16 PF in such a fashion as to give as bad an impression as possible. Construction and cross-validation proceeded in precisely the same manner as the MD scale. The Faking Bad scale, however, appeared to work a bit better. Using a cutting score of 6, 94% of the faked profiles were picked up by this scale, while none of the honestly answered profiles were picked up.

Scoring of the Faking Bad scale is done in precisely the same manner as that of the MD scale. It is again most convenient to make up a little scoring key, using the items and scoring directions shown in Table A-1. The score is simply the total of the number of items marked in the indicated direction.

The Random Scale

The Random scale was constructed by looking through 250 16 PF protocols for answers that were *infrequent* (O'Dell, 1971). The idea was that someone answering randomly would be much more likely to obtain tallies on each of these infrequent responses than someone answering honestly. Using a cutting score of 5 or greater, it was found that only 6% of normal records were called random with this score, while 86% of randomly answered records were correctly picked up. Further, Irvine and Gendreau (1974) found that this scale had an overall detection rate of 98% for students, and 87% with prison inmates.

This scale is slightly more difficult to score than the other two, for in order to make it work properly it was necessary to count alternatives that were answered as well as alternatives that were *not* answered. Thus, one needs two separate scoring keys, one to pick up the items which count if answered, and one to catch the items that count 1 if *not* answered. The items on the Random scale are listed in Table A-2, with the direction of scoring. Catching on to the scoring is a bit tricky, but one should do it rapidly. This scale is particularly useful if one is working with people whose motivation to cooperate is suspect.

TABLE A-2

ITEMS ON THE RANDOM SCALE

Items Which Count One if Answered in the Indicated Direction		Items Which Count One if *Not* Answered in the Indicated Direction	
Item	Direction	Item	Direction
4	c	1	a
12	b	2	a
20	b	28	b
23	b	29	a
38	a	53	b
51	b	112	a
52	b	116	c
54	a	128	b
66	b		
73	c		
77	a		
78	a		
80	a		
87	b		
91	b		
93	a		
102	a		
109	b		
118	a		
119	a		
121	a		
127	b		
143	a		

Source: O'Dell (1971). Copyright 1971 by the American Psychological Association. Reprinted by permission.

References

Cattell, R. B. *The description and measurement of personality.* Yonkers-on-Hudson, N.Y.: World Book Company, 1946.

Cattell, R. B. *Personality and motivation structure and measurement.* Yonkers-on-Hudson, N.Y.: World Book Company, 1957.

Cattell, R. B. *Personality and mood by questionnaire.* San Francisco: Jossey-Bass, 1973.

Cattell, R. B., Eber, H. W., & Tatsuoka, M. M. *Handbook for the Sixteen Personality Factor Questionnaire [16 PF].* Champaign, Ill.: Institute for Personality and Ability Testing, 1970.

Cattell, R. B., & Scheier, I. H. *The meaning and measurement of neuroticism and anxiety.* New York: Ronald Press, 1961.

Cattell, R. B., & Warburton, F. W. *Objective personality and motivation tests.* Champaign, Ill.: University of Illinois Press, 1967.

Delhees, K. H., & Cattell, R. B. *Manual for the Clinical Analysis Questionnaire.* Champaign, Ill.: Institute for Personality and Ability Testing, 1975.

Erikson, E. H. *Childhood and society.* New York: Norton, 1950.

Eysenck, H. *The structure of human personality.* London: Methuen, 1970.

Irvine, M. J., & Gendreau, P. Detection of the fake "good" and "bad" response on the Sixteen Personality Factor inventory in prisoners and college students. *Journal of Consulting and Clinical Psychology,* 1974, *42,* 465-466.

References

Irvine, M. J., Gendreau, P., & O'Dell, J. W. Validity data for 16 PF dissimulation studies. In press.

Karson, S. Second-order personality factors and the MMPI. *Journal of Clinical Psychology*, 1958, *14*, 313-315.

Karson, S. The Sixteen Personality Factor Test in clinical practice. *Journal of Clinical Psychology*, 1959, *15*, 174-176.

Karson, S. Validating clinical judgments with the 16 PF test. *Journal of Clinical Psychology*, 1960, *16*, 394-397.

Karson, S. Second-order personality factors in positive mental health. *Journal of Clinical Psychology*, 1961, *17*, 14-19.

Karson, S. Group psychotherapy with latency age boys. *International Journal of Group Psychotherapy*, 1965, *15*, 81-89.

Karson, S., & Haupt, T. D. Second-order personality factors in parents of child guidance clinical patients. *Multivariate Behavioral Research*, 1968, *3* (Special edition), 97-106.

Karson, S., & O'Dell, J. W. Is the 16 PF factorially valid? *Journal of Personality Assessment*, 1974, *38*, 104-114.

Karson, S., & Pool, K. B. The construct validity of the Sixteen Personality Factors Test. *Journal of Clinical Psychology*, 1957, *13*, 245-252.

Karson, S., & Pool, K. B. Second-order factors in personality measurement. *Journal of Consulting Psychology*, 1958, *22*, 299-303.

Karson, S., & Sells, S. B. Comments on Meehl and Rosen's paper. *Psychological Bulletin*, 1956, *53*, 335-337.

Karson, S., & Wiedershine, L. J. An objective evaluation of dynamically oriented group psychotherapy. *International Journal of Group Psychotherapy*, 1961, *11*, 166-174.

IPAT Staff. *Tabular Supplement No. 1 to the 16 PF Handbook*. Champaign, Ill.: Institute for Personality and Ability Testing, 1970.

IPAT Staff. *Manual for the 16 PF*. Champaign, Ill.: Institute for Personality and Ability Testing, 1972.

O'Dell, J. W. Method for detecting random answers on personality questionnaires. *Journal of Applied Psychology*, 1971, *55*, 380-383.

Winder, P., O'Dell, J. W., & Karson, S. New motivational distortion scales for the 16 PF. *Journal of Personality Assessment*, 1975, *39*, 532-537.

Index

New . . . The Karson Clinical Interpretation of the 16 PF

A computer analysis of Cattell's 16 Personality Factor Questionnaire (16 PF)

The *Karson Clinical Report,* developed by Dr. Samuel Karson, gives the psychologist, the psychiatrist, the psychiatric social worker, and the physician an easy-to-use report of the in-depth analysis of underlying personality dynamics in the clinician's language.

This four-page report features both narrative and charted descriptions and explores significant clinical findings and inferences. The narrative, written in a concise, compact style, provides a complete overview of the personality and clinical patterns. Charts give a visual display of scores in five significant areas: primary personality traits, clinical signs and syndromes, interpersonal patterns, cognitive factors, and need patterns.

The Karson Clinical Report combines a unique depth of clinical information with a simple-to-administer instrument. More than an initial report, the interpretation gives the significant information needed for diagnosis and treatment. The computer-generated report is complete without being cluttered.

The Karson Clinical Report is available from the Institute for Personality and Ability Testing, Inc., P. O. Box 188, Champaign, Illinois 61820. Contact IPAT for more information.